SEGUN ADEPOJU

Dwelling

In

God's Secret Place

... finding and enjoying the code to a full life.

Dwelling In God's Secret Place

June 2023

Author: Segun Adepoju

All rights reserved. This book or any parts thereof may not be reproduced in any form, stored in a retrieval system, or transmitted in any form by any means - electronic, mechanical, photocopy, recording or otherwise - without prior written permission of the Author, except as provided by United States of America copyright law.

Copyright © 2023 By Segun Adepoju

Contact: Segun Adepoju

Email: gettingunstuckwithmenow@gmail.com

Twitter: SegunAdepoju12

Printed in the United States of America

All scriptures quotations, unless otherwise indicated, are taken from the King James Version of the Holy Bible.

Dedication

This book is dedicated to:

- the glory of God
- the memory of my beloved later father, Prince Timothy Adepoju

and

- to my mother, Mrs. J. A. Adepoju for your prayers for me 24/7.

Acknowledgements

- My wife, Christy – for your support in many ways.

- Pastor (Dr.) Christy Ogbeide of Hope Kitchen Foundation, Houston, Texas – for your help in formatting this book.

Segun Adepoju
June, 2023.

Contents

Dedication   3

Acknowledgement   4

Introduction   7

Part One – Where is the Secret Place?

Chapter 1
The Secret Place   19

Chapter 2
The Way to the Secret Place   29

Chapter 3
Conditions to Abiding   37

Part Two – Sheltering Under God's Glory

Chapter 4
The Shadow of the Almighty   50

Chapter 5
The Glory and God's Shadow   63

Chapter 6
The Great Covering   77

Part Three – From Fear to Life

Chapter 7
Freedom from Fear – Weapon of Fear (Pt. 1) 92

Chapter 8
Freedom from Fear - Scriptural Panacea for
Overcoming Fear (Pt. 2) 103

Chapter 9
The Great Deliverance and Protection by God's
Angels 118

Part Four – The Abundant Life

Chapter 10
The Total Victory 130

Chapter 11
The Right Hand of God 140

Chapter 12
The Royal Dominion 150

Chapter 13
Blessed Assurance – The Right of Answered
Prayers 163

Chapter 14
Long Life and Salvation 178

Postscript 191

Index 197

Notes 206

Introduction

Moses and Psalm 91

> But it is not so with My servant Moses;
> He is entrusted *and* faithful in all My house. Num 12:7, AMP

> Now Moses was faithful in [the administration of] all God's house,
> [but only] as a *ministering* servant, [his ministry serving]
> as a testimony of the things which were to be spoken afterward [the revelation to come in Christ]; Heb 3:5, AMP

> Moses chose to sing the song God called him to sing.
> He faced incredible odds and
> challenges, but like Messiah,
> he led his people out of exile.
> He spoke with God, and
> despite several challenges,
> not knowing how or when,
> Moses trusted God. – Rabbi Jason Sobel[1]

The weekend of July 4, 2020 was one of those days when fatalities across the world peaked on account of Covid-19 pandemic which initially defied known scientific solutions. Fears were palpable on people's faces, literally. Deaths were as common as air. All you'd see on television channels and many social media was threat –

threat of death, sickness, hospitalization, job loss, etc.

For many, despite the apparent doom, they still had to go to work, shop at groceries, and visit loved ones when necessary. You were just unsure whether whatever safety protocols you chose - or the ones forced on you by the Governments and employers - would keep you safe. However smart you were, you were also not sure whether the safety protocols you chose would guarantee your safety.

Frankly, even after you've exhausted all known survival instincts, it took a lot of mental discipline to not think of death – or something close. People literally became prisoners of fears – whether openly or in their home recesses.

John Eldredge, in his great book, *Resilient*, aptly and dramatically described Covid-19 pandemic this way:

> To be suddenly stripped of your normal life; to live under the fear of suffering and death; to be bombarded with negative news; kept in a state of constant uncertainty about the future, with no clear view of the finish line; and to lose every human countenance behind a mask - may I point out that this is exactly the torment that terrorist regime use to break down prisoners psychologically and physically?[2]

Dwelling In God's Secret Place

The weekend under reference will be remembered for a long time. For me, it was supposed to be a short *quiet time* before I would begin a few house chores.

> ... though prayers are important to have safety, being in God's *secret place* is much more important.

I had prayed, read the Bible, and meditated on God's words. It was 8:30am. I wanted to pray more – for protection, guidance, direction, and whatever I could remember to pray about. Then, I suddenly developed a huge burden to pray some prayers that I had developed from Psalm 91. I had no idea that I would still be on Psalm 91 for the next five hours or so.

I realized that though prayers are important to have safety, being in God's *secret place* is much more important. You can pray amiss. And even if your prayers work you through a bout of safety from plagues or death, you'd still die one day, if the Lord Jesus tarries. But when you perpetually live in God's *secret place,* even if you die of Covid-19 or any other illness, you would not have died eternally.

So, by 1pm, I had written twenty pages in my journal, under God's inspiration. This led to the book in your hands.

MOSES WROTE PSALM 91

Psalm 91 is unique in many respects. Moses authored it. He was God's mouthpiece in the

> ... while Psalm 91 is a good confession prayer for divine protection ... It can't work for just anyone. It's neither an incantation nor a magic wand. It's not a fire brigade, hurry-and-recite, "go-to" talisman book to get immediate protection.

events that led to the liberation of the Israelites from their Egyptian overlords. Several plagues tormented the Egyptians while the Israelites and their livestock were unperturbed in Goshen. Moses was a man who had a first-hand experience of wanton destructions that befell Pharaoh and his armies in the Red Sea. He saw all of these! So, when Moses talks about divine protection, you'd better pay attention. What else do you expect from a man whose name was mentioned over eight hundred times in the Bible? He is the fourth most mentioned names in the Bible after David, God being the first and followed by Jesus Christ.

Moses was one of the greatest and humblest people who ever lived. He had long and short bouts of meetings with God in the past. There were times he had wonderful time (cool day) with God. There were also "not-so-good" times. He would be angry with God, and with the Israelites, even though he was a friend of God and God's confidante. He knew the importance of God's presence and that's why Psalm 91 matters to you, especially regarding its central theme – the *secret place*.

Moses also knew what it meant to follow God's direction and what it's like, to enjoy the benefits of God's direction. He knew the impending calamity that awaited any refusal to live in line with God's commandments.

A good example was Pharaoh, King of Egypt who refused to let go of the Israelites. Moses understood that God's *secret place* is a fortress where divine protection abounds. He experienced how God protected him and dealt fearfully with rebellious Korah, Dathan, and Abiram (Numbers chapter 16).

PSALM 91 IS UNIQUE

In my special encounter of July 4, 2020, I realized that, while Psalm 91 is a good confession prayer for divine protection, it's more than that. It can't work for just anyone. It's neither an incantation nor a magic wand. It's not a fire brigade, hurry-and-recite talisman's "go-to book" for immediate protection.

Psalm 91 is one of those Old Testament Scriptures that spoke of the salvation plan of God for mankind. It talks about the riches of living in the "eternity" of God even right from your earthly sojourn.

Psalm 91 cannot be totally detached from Psalm 90. In Psalm 90:1, Moses declared, "Lord, You have been our dwelling place in all generations." (NKJV). The Israelites had grumbled against God in the wilderness, and He had determined to wipe off that generation from age twenty. (See Numbers chapter 14:29). You will read more of this in chapter 14).

Again, in Psalm 91, Moses reiterated the certainty of God as the Israelites' "dwelling place" and that those who dwell this (secret) place would enjoy God's covering. But dwelling in this place would be conditioned upon loving what God loves and hating what He hates.

I can imagine the mind of God as a background to Psalm 91:

"Moses, remember how these people provoked me to anger by complaining and not believing or trusting me to do what I promised (that is, taking them to promise land). Recall how I promised to wipe off the adults among them, starting from age twenty and above. The future generations should however know that I am still the merciful God.

As a threshold, if those generations would continue to make me as their "dwelling place" and trust in my ability to save, then, I will be their covering and they would not waste away. I wrap myself in mystery and reveal myself and my plan to whoever I want and at the time I set...

"I have spoken and wouldn't change what I set to do to the complainants among them. But to those future generations, they need not be afraid of dying young or at 60, or at 70.

My plan for them is "long life – a life of rich fulfilment set and known by me alone, long enough for them to fulfil their respective purposes. And for them to be sure that all of these are not empty promises, I will let them experience my "salvation" ultimately."

I can further imagine Moses asking to know more about this long life that is "capped" with "salvation" and God refusing to tell him because it was not about him.

Jesus told His disciples in Mathew 13:16-17 and apostle Peter emphasized in I Peter 1:10-12 that the prophets and angels longed to "see" this salvation but because it wasn't meant for them, they were refrained from knowing it.

So, as a follow up to Psalm 90, Moses in Psalm 91:1 said, "He who dwells in the secret place of the Most High shall abide under the shadow of the Almighty." (NKJV).

The special words here are (i) "dwells," (ii) "secret

> In Hebrew, *Sether* means the hiding place, where to seek cover or protection, usually the caves and rocks.
>
> In Psalm 32:7, David called God his hiding place. He said, "Thou art my hiding place; thou shalt preserve me from trouble; thou shalt compass me about with songs of deliverance." Rock symbolizes Jesus Christ. (See I Corinthians 10:4; Acts 4:11, and Isaiah 28:16).
>
> The Hebrews' understanding of *Sether* is associated with God of the Israelites as their shelter and hiding place who would keep them from dangers and troubles.

place," (iii) Most High," (iv) "abide," and (v) "shadow." Everything else in Psalm 91 piggybacks these special words in verse one. Out of the five special words, the *secret place* is the central point.

The Hebrew word for *dwell* is *yashab* which means to reside in and *possess* a place with intention to live there.

The relevant questions then are, "where or what is the *secret place*? Is it physical? If it is, then, how many people can it possibly contain at a time? Is it on earth or in heaven?

If the *secret place* is physically on earth – such as mountains, hills, valleys, church auditoria, prayer rooms – then, what happens to your safety after you leave there? If it is in heaven, then, why would the rest of Psalm 91 matter to you, or anyone on earth? Afterall, in heaven, there won't be snare of the fowler, terrors, pestilences, evils and plagues. The promise of "long life" wouldn't matter, either.

Could the *secret place* be a form of spiritual or *positional* place? In other words, does the *"secret place"* refer to your status as a believer in God (and in Christ Jesus) at a given time?

Why would Moses use such a word? Why would he tie your *safety* to the *secret place*?

A hiding place could be physical, such as a stronghold, tower, shelter, or fortress where one can run into and find refuge, as was the case when the Philistines went to look for David.

When David heard about the Philistine's pursuit, he went down to the stronghold. (II Samuel 5:17). In our present dispensation however, is the *secret place* restricted to a physical location?

As stated earlier, Moses in Psalm 90:1 had addressed God as the "dwelling place" - a refuge, sanctuary, and stability - in all generations.

> The secret place in Psalm 91 ... is spiritual and positional.

The *secret place* in Psalm 91:1 thus speaks of more than a physical place. It's rather spiritual and positional. It describes your *positional status* when you make God your source and savior by surrendering to the lordship of Jesus Christ in genuine salvation.

Ephesians 1:3 tells us that God has blessed us in heavenly realms with every spiritual blessing in Christ and the rest of the chapters tells us the components of this blessing. But they remain *potential* and in the *heavenly realms* as long as we don't activate them with our faith in God.

GETTING READY FOR TRANSFORMATION

The main purpose of the knowledge and revelations that you will encounter in in this book is to transform you into a matured (disciplined) child of God who is prepared for life eternal.

Reading and digesting this book in your hands will redefine your life and values differently, but positively.

Getting meaningful results from reading and studying requires a lot of mental and physical disciplines and personal goal resetting.

You must prepare your mind to learn, unlearn and relearn new things. You need to study and reflect with an open mind so you can enjoy the flexibility of the Holy Spirit's guidance and inspiring words.

Let's get started.

Part One

Where is the Secret Place?

===========================

The purpose of a place determines eligibility for entrance, participation, and

transactions to be conducted there. A place that's designated for

habitation must be well-planned and protected.

Your safety

hangs around where and how you dwell. For example, the fetus' life

is intricately linked to the pregnant woman.

it enjoys necessary nutrients as long

as the placenta is there.

===========================

1

The Secret Place

"He who
dwells in the
secret place of the Most High
Shall abide under the shadow
of the Almighty. Psalm 91:1, NKJV

"... the priests always went into the first
part of the tabernacle, performing the services.
But into the second part the high
priest *went* alone once
a year ... the Holy Spirit indicating this, that the way
into
the Holiest of All was not yet made manifest while the
first
tabernacle was still standing. It *was* symbolic for the
present time
in which both gifts and sacrifices are offered which
cannot make him
who performed the service perfect in regard to the
conscience..." Hebrews 9:6-10. NKJV

A secret place is restricted; it's not open to everybody. It is usually opened by certain keys or codes that are restricted to a select group.

For clarity, a secret place isn't always dark and doesn't have to be so to keep people away. Besides, it's not every secret place that is negative or evil. It's the people and purpose of a place that make it evil or negative. For example, the "Holiest of All" in the Tabernacle was restricted and it wasn't negative. (See Hebrews 9:1-9).

EVERY KINGDOM HAS ITS SECRETS

Every kingdom has its 'dos' and 'don'ts.' God's kingdom is no exception. In Luke 10, Jesus taught the crowd about the kingdom of God through a parable of the Sower. His disciples didn't understand the parable.

Before telling them the meaning of the parable, Jesus said, "... To you [who have been chosen] it has been granted to know *and* recognize the mysteries of the kingdom of God, but to the rest it is in parables ..." (Luke 8:10, AMP). Here Jesus taught the crowd in parables, but He explained the meaning of the parable to the disciples. See Luke 8:11-15.

> The people "outside" can't understand the language and love of God.

God gave the chosen (disciples) the keys (secrets) of the kingdom of God. In this context therefore, the knowledge (meaning of the parable) is the *key* while the kingdom of God connotes the *secret (place)*.

Luke 17:20-21 says that the Kingdom of God isn't something you can see with naked eyes; its within you. If you are in God and He's in you, then, look no further to understand His kingdom. Romans 14:17 tells us that the kingdom of God is righteousness and peace and joy in the Holy Spirit. As you continue your earthly journey with Him, you continue in His kingdom when you get to heaven.

In John 17:3, Jesus said, "Now this is eternal life: that they may know You, the only true [supreme and sovereign] God, and [in the same manner know] Jesus [as the] Christ whom You have sent." (TLB). Here, knowledge of God is eternal life. Ecclesiastes 3:11 says that God has "... planted eternity [a sense of divine purpose] in the human heart [a mysterious longing which nothing under the sun can satisfy, except God] ..." (AMP).

The Holy Spirit will tell you about the secrets in God's Kingdom, if you let Him.

EVERYONE IS INVITED

Everyone is invited to be part of God's family but not everyone is in it.

In Matthew 22, Jesus gave a parable of a wedding banquet where there were two categories of invited guests - **selected invitees and anyone found on the street.**

The selected invitees were meant to be the original guests, but they refused to come. Those who were found on the street were the people invited when the select refused to honor the invitation. The King noticed a man at the banquet who was not wearing the wedding

> Life eternal begins with knowing God and continues through "living" His word in this phase of eternity on earth. It is a quality of life characterized by obedience to God and the fulfilment of His purpose.
>
> Death does not truncate or stop this eternal life; it's rather a means of transition to the next phase.

clothes. He ordered this non-compliant guest to be taken out and thrown into utter darkness, where there would be weeping and gnashing of teeth.

In that parable, the kingdom is God's family. The wedding ceremony connotes our being united with God through salvation when we come to Jesus in repentance.

The servants are the men and women of God like Moses, Elijah, Jeremiah, and a host of other servants of God.

The king's son is Jesus Christ. The wedding clothes refer to holiness. Hebrews 12:14 tells us that without holiness, no one will "see the Lord." At your ultimate "wedding" when your sojourn on earth ends, it's your washed, clean, and spotless "wedding clothes" (holiness) that you use as your key (or ticket, or right) to enter the marriage supper of the lamb. You would be clothed in a white robe as you would have escaped the corruption of this world. The Bible assures that, "Blessed are those who wash their robes, that they may have the right to the tree of life and may go through the gates into the city." (Rev 22:14, NIV).

To be sure, to enjoy the blessings of the *secret place* to the fullest, you must work out your salvation with "fear and trembling."

Not being born again is living outside of the *secret place*. The Bible says, "Outside are the dogs [the godless, the impure, those of low moral character] and the sorcerers [with their intoxicating drugs, and magic arts], and the immoral persons [the perverted, the molesters, and the adulterers], and the murderers, and the idolaters, and everyone who loves and practices lying (deception, cheating)." (Revelation 22:15, AMP). And if you're already part of this family, then you must "crucify" your flesh (sinful nature) with its passions and desires to sustain this status. (See Galatians 5:24).

WHY IS THE "PLACE" SECRET?

God is the head of the kingdom of God. He's covered with mystery and everything about Him is mystery except what He reveals. The salvation plan of God for mankind is a mystery. Revelation 3:8 tells us about the book of the lamb (Jesus being the lamb of God) and that this lamb was slain from "the foundation of the world." (NKJV).

According to Peter, this lamb "was manifest in these last times..." (I Pet 1:20). God kept this secret from those who killed Jesus. Apostle Paul was very direct. "... we declare God's wisdom, a mystery that has been hidden and that God destined for our glory before time began. None of the rulers of this age understood it, for if they had, they would not have crucified the Lord of glory." (I Cor 2:7-8).

In the classic conversation between the Jews and Jesus in John 8, the Jews had hard time believing that Jesus was from God much less believing that He was before Abraham whom they claimed as their father. Then Jesus told them what was too big a mystery to them: "Your father Abraham rejoiced to see my day: and he saw it, and was glad. Verily, verily, I say unto you, Before Abraham was, I am." (John 8:56 & 58). Even the cleansing by the blood of Jesus is a mystery. Praise God! Jesus is the wisdom of God!

Dwelling In God's Secret Place

The wisdom of the *secret place* is embodied in God's word, which is now manifested in Christ Jesus, and revealed to God's children by His Holy Spirit. Paul talked about this wisdom when he said. "But it was to us that God made known his secret by means of His Spirit. The Spirit searches everything, even the hidden depths of God's purposes." (I Cor 2:10, GNT).

> The *secret place is* ... not a "temple," "church facility," "mountains" or some physical locations where you merely pay homage to God.

God's family is positionally secret to those outside of the covenant relationship with Him, who have not surrendered to the lordship of Jesus, and who are still being ruled by their flesh and lustful appetites.

God had kept this secret from the past rulers of this world whose lack of understanding of this mystery led them to kill Jesus. Certainly, if they had known, then they wouldn't have crucified Jesus. Indeed, the precious salvation from God is a *secret place* that can only be accessed by those who are "washed and made clean" by the blood of Jesus, and who are led by the Spirit of God. That's why I Corinthians 2:10-12 tells us that:

> But we know about these things because God has sent his Spirit to tell us, and his Spirit searches out and shows us all of God's deepest

secrets... And no one can know God's thoughts except God's own Spirit. And God has actually given us his Spirit (not the world's spirit) to tell us about the wonderful free gifts of grace and blessing that God has given us. (TLB).

What verse 10 calls "deepest secrets" are explained in verse 12 to be "wonderful free gifts of grace and blessing that God has given us" which is another way of explaining our salvation.

The secret place of the Most High described by Moses in Psalm 91:1 connotes the sacredness of *God's dwelling* characterized by joy, safety, and protection from fear and storms. As captured by the Sons of Korah, "... we will not be afraid...There is a river that brings joy to the city of God, to the sacred house of the Most High. God is in that city, and it will never be destroyed;" (Ps 46:2-5, GNT).

The *secret place* is a figurative expression and not necessarily a physical place – not a "temple," "church facility," "mountains" or some physical locations where you merely pay homage to God. If it were, every Dick, Tom and Harry would just run there for protection, even without good relationship with God born out of genuine salvation.

The secret place is a metaphorical description of God's house and the expression of salvation in the person of Christ. You must 'dwell" in this secret place before you could "abide under God's shadow." In other words, to have access to and fully enjoy divine glory and protection, you must be a member of the household of God.

SOMETHING TO THINK ABOUT

Reflection Point	Have you "washed your robes and made them white" and pure? Are you daily working out your salvation to maintain and sustain your status as a child of God?
Scripture Focus	**Revelation 22:14** - Blessed (happy, prosperous, to be admired) are those who wash their robes [in the blood of Christ by believing and trusting in Him—the righteous who do His commandments], so that they may have the right to the tree of life, and may enter by the gates into the city. (AMP).

Note
_____
_____
_____
_____

Segun Adepoju

2

The Way to the Secret Place

> Jesus said to him,
> "I am the [only] Way [to God]
> and the [real] Truth and
> the [real] Life; no one comes to the
> Father but through Me. John 14:6
> (AMP).

Every normal house has an entrance door.

A house without a door is next to nothing; it soon becomes a cover for reptiles, rodents, and wild animals. After a while, it becomes a jungle and if you call that a house, that may be right, but certainly not a house where normal people dwell.

Recall that in chapter 1, we discussed about the *secret place connoting* God's house or God's family through salvation in Christ Jesus. God's *secret place,* even though very large, has one door.

THE "DOOR," THE "WAY," AND THE "GATE" TO GOD'S HOUSE

The "Door" means the same as the "Way," and the "Gate." They refer to Jesus Christ. Jesus is *the* Door to God's house. In His own words, Jesus said, "I am the Door; anyone who enters through Me will be saved [and will live forever], and will go in and out [freely], and find pasture (spiritual security)." (Jn 10:9, AMP).

The definite article *"the"* shows exclusivity – that Jesus is "the only Door" to God and to His family. In other words, *anyone who enters God's house through Jesus Christ will be saved.*

The "pasture" in John 10:9

> Even though the "Holy Place" where God dwells as stated in Hebrews chapter 10 might mean heaven, it's your salvation that creates a pathway of sonship relationship here on earth and which leads to God in heaven.

typifies sustenance made available by God's divine power, which, according to 2 Peter 1:3-4 (AMP), gives you "everything necessary" to live a life of fulfillment of purpose. To be clear, "entering through me" connotes *salvation through him (Jesus).* This scripture literally summarizes Psalm 91 because it has conditions to dwelling in God's house and the attendant benefits (blessings).

Interestingly, in John 14, Jesus offered a great comfort and assured that there are many mansions in His father's house (verse 2) and unequivocally stated that He's "the [only] Way [to God]" (verse 6, AMP). In effect, the "Door" and the "Way" in John 10:9 and John 14:6 respectively, are pointing to the one and only entrance to God's house – Jesus Christ. Hebrew 10:20 calls this "new and living way…"

Whether you refer to Him as the Door, the Way, or the Gate, the important signal that characterizes Him as the only path to God is that it is narrow.

The Way is not broad because it involves self-denial, discipline, faith in God and obedience to Him. Again, this aligns with some of the conditions in Psalm 91 such as having to dwell in the secret place (verse 1), making the Lord as your refuge and your dwelling place (verse 9), and setting your love on God (verse 14).

> Jesus is life-giving because He is *the* life. Life here doesn't mean being alive but having a life while alive, full of purpose and continuing in life eternal hereafter.

The Bible says, "You can enter God's Kingdom only through the narrow gate… But the gateway to life is very narrow and the road is difficult, and only a few ever find it." (Matt 7:13-14, NLT).

The interesting thing here is that you have the power of choice to choose the "Door" today, and in fact, now! And if you have chosen it before but you're now "one-leg-in and one-leg-out" or totally living independently of the Way, or altogether unsure of your path any longer, then, you can begin anew and again, now. Let me motivate you for a better choice with the following words from the Book of Hebrews which says:

> Therefore, believers, since we have confidence *and* full freedom to enter the Holy Place [the place where God dwells] by [means of] the blood of Jesus, by this new and living way which He initiated *and* opened for us through the veil [as in the Holy of Holies], that is, through His flesh, and since we have a great *and* wonderful Priest [Who rules] over the house of God, let us approach [God] with a true *and* sincere heart in unqualified assurance of faith, having had our hearts sprinkled *clean* from an evil conscience and our bodies washed with pure water. Let us seize *and* hold tightly the confession of our hope without wavering, for He who promised is reliable *and* trustworthy *and* faithful [to His word]. Hebrews 10:19-23, AMP.

There's a useful nexus between John 14:4-6 and Hebrews 10 quoted above. In John 14:4-6, Jesus asked whether the disciples knew the way to the "place" He was going to "prepare." Thomas said that they didn't know where Jesus was going, how much less the way. Then Jesus stated that

He's the Way, the Truth, and the life. No one could go to God except through Him.

Even though the "Holy Place" where God dwells as stated in Hebrews 10 might mean heaven, it's your salvation that creates a pathway of sonship relationship here on earth that leads to God in heaven.

LIVE YOUR LIFE IN ME

In John 15:7, Jesus said that, if you remain in Him and His words remain in you, you may ask for anything you want, and it will be granted. Here, your answered prayers are conditioned upon your *abiding in Jesus Christ* which connotes obedience to His instructions. He is the connector and link to God; He knows what to do to make your prayers reach God. He is the Way to God. In the times of the Apostles, His teachings, and doctrines, in addition to himself, used to be referred to as the "Way" or the "Way of God." See Acts of the Apostles 9:2; 18:26; 19:9, 23; 22:4, and 24:14.

> ... anyone who enters God's house through Jesus Christ will be saved.

Jesus is the *only* Door to God's house, pass through Him and you'll meet and experience God.

Jesus is the *only Way* leading to God's house, follow Him and you won't be astray. God's house is full of treasures where you have rest and peace. Jesus is the *only Gate leading to the treasures in it*. The Gate is still open.

Man is finite, limited, and fizzles away with time. Human beings often promise much but either deliver little or none. Deception, uncertainties, confusions, and envies often characterize man's way, and in most cases, man's ways are opposed to God's way. Isaiah 55:8 says that God's thoughts are not your thoughts, and that your ways are different from His.

You may have lovely titles, accolades, honors, and endowments, these are no substitutes for directions to God. You may be a pastor, or prophet, or bishop, titles aren't absolute in man's pursuit of God. The only faultless Way where spiritual robbers and danger men would not waylay and eliminate you, is Jesus Christ.

Though narrow, the Gate assures of the greatest protection, security, and safety. Indulgence that is afforded by the broad gates may provide pleasure to the body and soul. The substance of the narrow Gate however is discipline which not only prolongs the body and animates the soul but also feeds your spirit unto eternal nourishment.

The value of a house determines the cost or quality of the door. You don't hang a rickety five hundred dollar-door on a million-dollar house full of golden materials.

In the *secret place* we have spiritual and physical protection from all hazards and dangers. We also have prosperity, and calming assurance of safety during storms of life. In God's house is eternal salvation for mankind and it's important for God to seal it with Jesus' blood. Blood symbolizes life because the life of a thing is in its blood. Who else offers such a life with his blood? Absolutely none except Jesus Christ!

> Maturity is the fruit of discipline and those who feed on it not only grow strong, but also become godly. The Scriptures tells us that godliness (spiritual trainings) is of value in everything and in every way, since it holds promise for the present life and for the life to come. (I Timothy 4:8, AMP).

SOMETHING TO THINK ABOUT

Reflection Point	Attending church or programs or "Christian" services, though important, is not the absolute way of finding God through the

	Way. Neither is bearing "Christian" names!
Scripture Focus	**II Corinthians 13:5** – "Test *and* evaluate yourselves *to see* whether you are in the faith *and* living your lives as [committed] believers. Examine yourselves [not me]! Or do you not recognize this about yourselves [by an ongoing experience] that Jesus Christ is in you—unless indeed you fail the test *and* are rejected as counterfeit?" (AMP).

Note

3

Conditions to Abiding

> My eyes will be on the faithful (honorable) of the land, that they may dwell with me; He who walks blamelessly is the one who will minister to *and* serve me."
> Ps 101:6, AMP

Conditions are factors that determine or influence the outcome of a thing.

Whether in simple contracts or in man's relationship with the spiritual, certain promises, oaths, and covenants are intricately tied to meeting certain standards or fulfilling some obligations.

Hebrews 12:14 tells us that we must pursue peace with all people and be holy before we can see the Lord. The pursuit of peace and being holy are conditions while seeing the Lord (experiencing the goodness of the Lord while on earth and living with the Lord in life hereafter) is the reward or blessing. Similarly, Psalm 101:6 tells

> When you love God, you'd love your fellow human beings.

us, "My eyes will be on the faithful (honorable) of the land, that they may dwell with me; He who walks blamelessly is the one who will minister to *and* serve me." (AMP). Thus, to "dwell in the secret place," you must be faithful to all that God has put within your reach.

The blessings in Psalm 91 are not without conditions. The *secret place* is so important that we must touch on conditions attached to experiencing its blessings.

PSALM 91 CONDITIONS

In Psalm 91, we see three basic conditions which are in verses 1, 9, and 14. Let's briefly talk about them.

1.   Dwelling in secret place - Verse 1 says that he who dwells in the secret place of the most High shall abide under the shadow of the Almighty. So, you must "dwell" in the *secret place* first and then enjoy all that it offers. Happily, we have talked about this in chapter 1. You may want to read and conduct further studies until you master its nuances.

2.   Making God your habitation – Verses 9 and 10 say that because you have made the Lord your *habitation*, no evil shall befall you, neither shall any plague come near your dwelling. In other words, making the Lord your habitation comes first, then you have the blessing of divine protection. "Habitation" here means, among other things, refuge, shelter, dwelling, which all collectively connote a place of protection – a covering from danger, harsh weather, heat, or cold.

Making the Lord your habitation means that you make a conscious effort to seek the Lord's help. You must do the "making" deliberately and purposely. *There are times when life's hardships offer you alternatives which appear alluring, easy to grasp, fun to embrace, and too good to be ignored. At those times, who do you seek first for help? Where does your trust lie – man or God? On whom is your hope built?*

Psalm 147 talks at length about God's power of deliverance, about his goodness to those who hope in Him, and His pleasure for those who fear Him. Verses 10 and 11 say that "His pleasure is not in strong horses, nor his delight in brave soldiers; but he takes pleasure in those who honor him, in those who trust in his constant love." (GNT). Thus, making the Lord your habitation connotes trusting in Him, fearing Him, believing in Him, and hoping in Him for help and whatever it is that you need. The good news is that "God is our shelter and strength, always ready to help in times of trouble." (Psalm 46:1, GNT).

3.   Setting your love on God – Verse 14 says, "Because he hath set his love upon me, therefore will I deliver him: I will set him on high, because he hath known my name." Here, loving God and knowing his name are the conditions while deliverance and divine lifting are the rewards.

Genuine love comes from a sincere heart. See I Timothy 1:5.

Christian Standard Bible's rendition of Psalm 91:14 says, "Because he has his heart set on me…" In effect, you've got to set your delight, affection, longing, and care on God to enjoy His blessings. You must love God without reservation. His command is quite clear: "…love the Lord your God with all your heart and mind and with all your soul and with all your strength [your entire being]." (Deut 6:5, AMP).

Setting your love on God requires the totality of your being. It connotes giving Him your undivided attention, being faithful and committed to His causes. And these should always find expressions in your services to and worship of Him.

Setting your heart on God separates you from the likes of the Pharisees and Sadducees, the religious bigots who focus on outward appearances and not the state of the heart. You want to be like David who led his people according to the integrity of his heart. (See Psalm 72:78 and I Kings 9:4).

When you love God, you'd love your fellow human beings; you would serve Him by serving others; you would not hurt Him by practicing sinning (that is, by making sinning a habit). When you love God, you'd worship Him with all of you and all you've got! At this point, He would accept you and your offerings. Your problems become His "problems."

NOTES ON THE CONDITIONS

A quick look at the verses of Psalm 91 that have conditions in them tend to show that the blessings in those verses attach solely to the conditions there. But a deeper reflection would unfold that the blessings that follow or that are in the verses with conditions are cumulative and apply to all the conditions.

For example, it would be wrong to assume that once you make the Lord your habitation, all that you have is the blessings of verses 10 to 13 and no more. It's not so! *To be clear, the three conditions in verses 1, 9, and 14 point to one and only requirement, and that is a genuine salvation.* But to fully enjoy the package, you must *continue* to work out your salvation with fear and trembling. (See Philippians 2:12). And don't be afraid that you might get it wrong in your endeavors at working this out. It's God who helps you to do what is godly. He will direct and sustain you because "it is God who works in you to will and to act in order to fulfill his good purpose." (Philippians 2:13).

> Even if God chooses not to treat you as you deserve, the world is full of different evil spirits that can influence your words, for or against you.

You should not rest on your oars or fold your arms and expect things to just happen the way you want it without lifting hands and limbs. *You've got to work, pray, have healthy relationships with people, dare, and venture.* For example, if you have genuine salvation, then you have fulfilled Psalm 91:1. But don't stop there. Verse 2 says, "I will say of the LORD, "He is my refuge and my fortress, my God, in whom I trust." This shows that you must say good things that you want, to complement what you do.

Three things are worthy of note in verse 2, namely, (i) what you say, (ii) to whom you speak and (iii) the relationship you keep with the audience.

(i)   *What you say* – The things you say have a direct and important impact on your life and how you live. To enjoy your salvation to the fullest, you must say what is helpful and edifying. (See Ephesians 4:29).

The connection between your heart and your mouth isn't only anatomical but also psychological and spiritual. You tend to act what you say, most times.

At a certain time, the Israelites grumbled against Moses and Aaron. In fact, they started saying harsh words against themselves: "... "If only we had died in Egypt! Or in this wilderness! Why is the LORD bringing us to this land only to let us fall by the sword...?" (Number 14:2-3, NIV). In verse 27, God told Moses and Aaron, "... How long will this wicked community grumble against me? I have heard the complaints of these grumbling Israelites."

> The Way is not broad because it involves self-denial, discipline, faith in God and obedience to Him.

The Israelites grumbled against God and said harsh words, and God called them wicked. And here's God's verdict that has bearing on what you might be saying while in tough times, especially if it questions God's omnipotence. "... 'As surely as I live, declares the Lord, I will do to you the very thing I heard you say." (Verse 28, NIV). What did they say? See verses 2 and 3 mentioned above.

Then God continued in verse 29: "In this wilderness your bodies will fall—every one of you twenty years old or more who was counted in the census and who has grumbled against me." (NIV). This is what they used their mouths to confess in verse 2.

Even if God chooses not to treat you as you deserve, the world is full of different evil spirits that can influence your words, for or against you. Proverbs 13:3 says, "the one who guards his mouth [thinking before he speaks] protects his life; The one who opens his lips wide [and chatters without thinking] comes to ruin." (AMP). Wisdom, maturity, and a good life begin with what you say.

(ii)   *Saying of the Lord* – Sometimes, what you say isn't as important as your audience. For instance, what you tell your friends and get away with, might land you in trouble if you say it to the President of the United States.

In Psalm 91:2, Moses did not muster some idle words to an irresponsible fellow. He said, "I will say of the LORD...." To fully enjoy the package of your salvation, you must pray to the Lord – the one and only God Almighty. He knows what you need and when you need it. Don't say harsh words against God while in distress. Learn from the Israelites in Numbers chapter 14. Both Moses and the stubborn Israelites' generation spoke to God but what they said determined their place in God's judgment.

In Numbers 14:2-3, the Israelites said harsh words to God but in Psalm 91:2, Moses told God good words he expected to have.

(ii)   *The relationship* – In the battles of life, what often determines our defeat or victory isn't what we do as much as who is with us. *When the war is fiercer than anticipated, soldiers at the warfront would call for reinforcement. With the right strategies and intelligence, reinforcement increases the chance of victory by a wide margin. When God is with us in distress, victory is assured.*

Prophet Isaiah spoke of spiritual reinforcement in this way, "Associate yourselves, O ye people, and ye shall be broken into pieces ... Take counsel together, and it shall come to nought; speak the word, and it shall not stand: for God is with us." (Is 8:9-10).

Moses clearly reveals the nature of his relationship with God when he said, "He is my refuge and my fortress, my God, in whom I trust." What about you? Who is God, to you? Is He someone you run to only when you're stuck or your permanent habitation?

PATHWAY TO ANSWERED PRAYERS

It's not everyone who calls on God that gets answers. Only those who call on Him through or in the name (character) of Jesus Christ with godly and pure motives get answers to their prayers.

> When God is with us in distress, victory is assured.

God instructed King Saul to go and attack the Amalekites and *totally* destroy everything that belonged to them. Saul, however, was clever by half and reasoned that the best of sheep and cattle could be materials for sacrifice. He then spared them. He also spared their king, Agag. His intention was more like *worshipping* God with *fruits of disobedience.* God rejected Saul as a King. (See I Samuel 15:19-23).

To live in disobedience to God's words places you outside of God's family. As you know, a person who lives outside the covering of a shelter is in a precarious state and at the risk of all manners of dangers. He does not have the right to the trees of life which God had planted to heal His family members. The Bible says:

> Outside are the dogs [the godless, the impure, those of low moral character] and the sorcerers [with their intoxicating drugs, and magic arts], and the immoral persons [the perverted, the molesters,

and the adulterers], and the murderers, and the idolaters, and everyone who loves and practices lying (deception, cheating). Revelations 22:15, AMP.

Safety and covering in the *secret place* are in our obedience to and compliance with terms and conditions attached to it. See John 15:7

SOMETHING TO THINK ABOUT

Reflection Point	Total obedience to God is the secret of divine blessings.
Scripture Focus	**II Corinthians 10:3-6** – "For though we live in the world, we do not wage war as the world does. The weapons we fight with are not the weapons of the world. On the contrary, they have divine power to demolish strongholds. We demolish arguments and every pretension that sets itself up against the knowledge of God, and we take captive every thought to make it obedient to Christ. And we will be ready to punish every act of disobedience, once your obedience is complete. (NIV).

Segun Adepoju

Note

Part Two

Sheltering Under the Glory

============

We live in a rat race generation that is full of speed without destination; pleasure without responsibility; noise without voice; creed without penitence; motions without direction; programs without orderliness, and activities without purpose. Do not be caught up in the world's gummy maze of inconsistencies. God's glory doesn't cover for fun, or for no reason. It's to help you fulfil His purpose!

============

4

The Shadow of the Almighty

He who dwells in the secret place
of the Most High, Shall abide under the
shadow of the Almighty. Ps. 91:1, NKJV

The righteous shall flourish like the palm tree:
he shall grow like a cedar in Lebanon. Those that be
planted in the house of the Lord shall flourish in the
courts of our God. Ps 92:12-13

May you be richly rewarded by the Lord, the God of
Israel, under whose wings you have come to take
refuge. Ruth 4:12, NIV

> In Agriculture, crop husbandry is not always interesting, especially when the weather is harsh. Farming in some parts of Africa is a good example. The weather in most tropical agricultural areas is unpredictable which often makes most farmers to proactively find ways of providing alternative survival mechanisms for the nascent seedlings.

Dwelling In God's Secret Place

This is especially for cash crops such as cocoa and kola nuts, and food crops such as tomatoes and pepper seedlings. Irrigation is a viable alternative but it's best suited for mechanized as opposed subsistent farming which is predominant in many parts.

When you want to transfer the nascent soft seedlings from the nursey beds and sink (plant) them into their separate holes, you want to be sure that there's a prospect of shadow nearby as excessive heat from sunshine could destroy them. They can't withstand the heat because they are not used to being so exposed. They no longer have this luxury once relocated.

Some experienced farmers would plant cocoa seedlings near grown trees or very close to a yard of banana trees with the prospect that the tender seedlings would tap sufficient moisture from the ever-moisture banana roots.

There's also the hope that banana leaves would provide a shade for the young plants when the sun heat becomes excessive.

SHADOW OF THE ALMIGHTY

I am not sure of your exposure to, and understanding of agriculture, but the above analogy paints a picture of what happens when we dwell under the cover of God's glory. Throughout different seasons of life, our safety, protection, and survival are guaranteed.

There must be an original object and light reflection to have shadow. In other words, the object comes first. Your alignment to the direction of His light determines your level of covering. You must be in God before you can enjoy the blessings of His covering. *Jesus Christ is the tree of righteousness whose fortress gives us succor and protection.* He's the Tree of Life. When the "sun at midday" bites harder, we are secured. And when the ground is hard, or becomes rough and untillable, we tap our nutrients and strength from the Tree of Life and our roots become firm and established.

Jesus tells us that we should remain (abide) in him so He could remain in us and that, apart from Him, we cannot bear fruit. (John 15:4). The Bible tells us that righteous people are blessed because "they are strong, like a tree planted by a river. The tree produces fruit in season, and its leaves don't die. Everything they do will succeed." (Psalm 1:3, NCV).

Dwelling In God's Secret Place

As a member of God's family, you must acknowledge that God is your source and that your ultimate growth and success depend on His nurturing, covering and protection.

When you step on the shadow cast by heavy foliage in warm summer weather, you'd feel the diminished impact of heat. The shadow in Psalm 91:1 is a symbol of the covering and protection of God. Your salvation has placed you under God's covering. That's why you can confidently enjoy the promise: "There shall no evil befall thee, neither shall any plague come nigh thy dwelling." (Verse 10).

David understood the importance of God's covering. He said that one thing he would seek after was to dwell in the house of the Lord all the days of his life, to behold the beauty of the Lord. He believed that he would be safe in God's dwelling and that the Lord would hide him in the secret of His Tabernacle where God would set him high. (Ps 27:5-6).

> The extent of your growth depends on your attachment to and alignment with God's covering afforded by His glory.

Segun Adepoju

SHADOW OF GOD'S WINGS

In Exodus 19:4, God talked about how He carried the Israelites and brought them to Himself (to His mountain) as eagles would carry their young ones.

> Jesus Christ is also the "sun of righteousness." (Malachi 4:2). According to Psalm 92:12, the righteous shall flourish like a palm tree, growing like cedar in Lebanon. Verse 13 says, "those that be planted in the house of the Lord shall flourish in the courts of our God."
>
> As chlorophyll allows plants to absorb energy from light, we receive spiritual energy to flourish when we position ourselves in the direction of the light that the "sun of righteousness" gives. This light gives healing, restoration, and direction. It reflects on you and produces a righteousness which makes you "shine forth as the sun in the kingdom" of your Father. (Mathhew 13:43).

The eaglets have no capacity to fly on their own. They must totally entrust their safety to their mother's wings by cleaving. The mother eagle's right and left wings would stretch upside, creating some hollow space where the eaglets could tightly find their grip and protection from multi-directional turbulence. Simply put, the eaglet's safety does not come on its own but entirely from its mother.

When it comes to diving and maneuvering in space, eagles are unrivalled birds. They are God's masterpiece among the animals. A bald eagles' wingspan varies from 6 to 9ft. The feathers are incredibly crafted in an aerodynamic shape and designed for balancing in navigation and soaring. Regarding tender care toward their young ones, they are superb. As to strength and capacity, they are unique. It is not surprising that the Bible says that those who wait upon the Lord shall renew their strength, mounting up with wings like eagles, running without being weary, and walking without fainting. (See Isaiah 40:31).

God "carried" the Israelites from Egypt through the wilderness to the promise land. Israelites were slaves in Egypt, but God delivered them miraculously such that they had no input in the process. Similarly, we were all slaves to sin, but God delivered us through Jesus Christ's blood and His vicarious death.

We have no boast in our righteousness or in our salvation. God entirely put all the sufferings and death that we deserved on Jesus who took and nailed them to the cross. Somehow, Exodus 19:4 is a foreshadowing of what God manifested in Christ to "carry us into Himself" – by the work of salvation that integrates us into members of His family. It's worth celebrating!

You were dead in sins, and your sinful desires were not yet cut away. Then he gave you a share in the very life of Christ, for he forgave all your sins, and blotted out the charges proved against you, the list of his commandments which you had not obeyed. He took this list of sins and destroyed it by nailing it to Christ's cross. In this way God took away Satan's power to accuse you of sin, and God openly displayed to the whole world Christ's triumph at the cross where your sins were all taken away. Col 2:13-15, TLB.

David caught the revelation of divine protection afforded by the "shadow" of God's wings" and found a great solace in it. When he fled into the cave to escape king Saul's fierce pursuit, he pleaded for God's mercy and stated, "I will take refuge in the shadow of your wings until the disaster has passed." (Ps. 57:1, NIV). He likened Saul's pursuit to a "disaster " from which he needed refuge. God truly preserved him under his wing and consequently in verse 13, he testified, "For you have delivered me from death and my feet from stumbling, that I may work before God in the light of life." (NIV).

> God "carried" the Israelites from Egypt through the wilderness to the promise land... such that they had no input in the process.

In Ruth 1:16, Ruth refused to back out despite Naomi's repeated demands to go her separate ways. Ruth told her mother-in-law who was a Jew, "... Your people will be my people and your God my God." Ruth's unique step of faith eventually led her to meet Boaz, one of the kinsman-redeemers of her in-law's household.

In Ruth 4:12, Boaz told Ruth, "...May you be richly rewarded by the Lord, the God of Israel, under whose wings you have come to take refuge." (NIV). Oh yes, Boaz's prayer was answered; he "redeemed" Ruth who became his wife. The union produced Obed, Jesse, and David who all became grandparents to Joseph, the *father* of Jesus Christ.

COVENANT SPEAKS THROUGH THE SHADOW

In Psalm 46, the sons of Korah boldly affirmed the protection in the secret place when they said, "God is our shelter and strength, always ready to help in times of trouble." (v 1, GNT). A closer look at the rest of the verses in Psalm 46 reveals that when you're covered under God's shadow in the secret place, you're protected from all the negatives and evils that ordinarily plague mankind.

Let's look at some critical benefits of God's covering in Psalm 46.

- You will not fear, even in the face of global destruction. Afterall, when your earthly journey ends, eternal life hereafter is guaranteed. (v 2-3).

- Because you're dwelling "in the holy place where the Most High dwells, God's presence will not make you fall. (v 4-5).

- Because of God's presence, God's voice will resist every sound of intimidation that might emanate from catastrophes that shake nations, places, and kingdoms. (v 6).

- Because covenant works in a transgenerational way, you become a beneficiary of the blessings afforded by God's covenant with Jacob. (v 7). Remember God's covenant of fruitfulness with Jacob. (See Genesis 35:9-15).

- When God defends you, He leaves traces of evidence to show only what He can do. (v 8).

- For your sake, God destroys the source of Devil's strength (Devil's weapons) and uses His supreme power to stop all battles against you. (v 9).

- You and God can't be fighting the same battle at the same time. Because He's the one in charge of His *house,* you would not need to fight when He's fighting your battles. He wants to show Himself "supreme among the nations, supreme over the world." (v 10).

For emphasis, God's blessings that accompany His covenant with Jacob are with you. (v 11). God instructed Jacob to depart and settle in Bethel. Jacob and his household got rid of foreign gods and obeyed God. Then God's blessing of fruitfulness followed Jacob's obedience. (See Genesis 35:1-14).

God promised His people in Leviticus 26 that He would reward their obedience. One of the ways He would reward is to "remember" His covenant with Jacob, Isaac and with Abraham. (See Leviticus 26:42).

We live in a world that is full of evils. It's unthinkable how the world would have been without God's divine protection. God's covenant embedded in salvation is sealed with His word which ultimately affords the protection that Psalm 91 is talking about. Psalm 74:20 says, "Have respect to the covenant; For the dark places of the earth are full of the haunts of cruelty."

The covenant that Asaph was talking about in Psalm 74:20 is the one made with Abraham, and which continues till date. Asaph and his people had suffered in the hands of their captors and lost their protections to disobedience to God's words. Then they appealed to God to remember

His covenant. (See God's covenant with Abram, as he then was, in Genesis 15:13-14).

At a time, God determined to punish the nations that had held the Israelites captive in waterless pit. He then promised to receive the Israelites back and bless them twice for the troubles they had suffered. But before doing this, He had to remember His covenant first. God said, "... I have delivered you from death in a waterless pit because of the covenant I made with you, sealed with blood." (Zach 9:11-12, TLB).

> Somehow, Exodus 19:4 is a foreshadowing of what God manifested in Christ to "carry us into Himself" — by the work of salvation that integrates us into members of His family.

May God remember His covenant and deliver you from everything that holds you down.

> The same shadow of God's wings that towered as a refuge for Moses was the same that protected David from Saul's deadly arrow, and was the same that rewarded Ruth's step of faith and protected her from shame.

> The same is still alive to protect you from anything that is a threat to you. Hebrew 13:8 says Jesus Christ the same yesterday, today and ever more.
>
> Moses, David, Ruth, and a host of others who benefited from divine protection trusted in and prayed to God. (See Psalm 36:7).

SOMETHING TO THINK ABOUT

Reflection Point	We live in a world that is full of dangers and wickedness. Our fate isn't better than seedlings exposed to heat in the desert if we live apart from God's covering. Are you planted by the tree of life, or you are just on your own?
Scripture of the Day	Psalm. 57:1 - "I will take refuge in the shadow of your wings until the disaster has passed." (Ps. 57:1, NIV). Revelation 22:14 - "Blessed (happy, prosperous, to be

admired) are those who wash their robes [in the blood of Christ by believing and trusting in Him—the righteous who do His commandments], so that they may have the right to the tree of life, and may enter by the gates into the city." (AMP).

Note

5

The Glory and God's Shadow

> Jesus said to
> her, "Did I not
> say to you that if you
> believe [in Me], you will see
> the glory of God [the expression of
> His excellence]? Jn 11:40, AMP.

> Lift up your heads, O gates, And be lifted up, ancient doors, That the King of glory may come in. Ps 24:7

> But You, O LORD, are a shield for me,
> My glory [and my honor], and the One who lifts my head. Ps 3:3, AMP.

God lives in glory and is full of glory.

God's presence radiates glory and exudes the splendor of His majesty. Where you see God, His manifestation, or His Spirit, you will experience His glory.

It's God's glory that sets Him apart from everything else. Glory is attached to the saints and many things, except the devil. We have the glory of the sun, of the star, and of the moon. (1 Corinthians 15:41). We also have the glory of the saints. The devil, however, cannot have glory because he is intrinsically bereft of any virtue that produces it.

THE ULTIMATE PURPOSE OF GOD'S GLORY

The word "glory" comes from the Greek word, *doxa,* which could mean splendor, majesty, or grandeur.

While *glory* is used in general sense to describe honor, beauty, and fame, but when used in connection with God or His acts, it describes a manifestation or settling of His presence.

> Jesus reflected God's glory as mirror reflects an object.

Sometimes, the settling comes with smoke, fire, or thick clouds all of which produce awe that makes everyone reference Him. This was the case prior to God declaring the Ten Commandment on Mt. Sinai. (Exodus 19:9-25). God's glory also settled on the tabernacle upon completion by Moses. (Exodus 40:34-38).

The settling of God's glory was and is never for no reason. Direction and guidance, protection, instructions, and deliverance all come with it. Being the Yahweh Sabaoth (The Lord of Host of heaven), His glorious presence can fight and win for you. The Bible tells us that the Lord mighty in battle is the king of glory. (Psalm 24:7-8). And just to mention, God's glory is exclusively reserved for Him and cannot be shared. See Isaiah 42:8. But He can shine His glory upon you as a mark of His love for you.

Hebrews 1:3 tells us that Jesus Christ (the Son of God) is the "radiance of God's glory and the exact representation of his being..." (NIV). Jesus reflected God's glory as mirror reflects an object.

John 1:14 says, "And the Word was made flesh, and dwelt among us, (and we beheld his glory, the glory as of the only begotten of the Father,) full of grace and truth." Here, John the Baptist testified that he was part of the people who "saw," or "beheld" Jesus' glory. This glory (of Jesus) is full of grace and truth. And to be sure that this glory did not just appear to dazzle humanity but to birth an experience of divine blessings, verse 16 tells us that from Jesus' fullness of grace, we have received blessings upon blessings.

The reality is that we see God in Jesus Christ and vice versa. The Amplified Version renders it that Jesus "... has explained Him [and interpreted and revealed the awesome wonder of the Father]." (Jn 1:18, AMP). Through transforming experiences in God's family, you can see God in action through encounters which Jesus Christ (and His words). And that would be sufficient explanation of God's glory, even though God remains unseen physically.

Manifestations of God's glory produces certain experiences of reference and worship which birth transformation that conforms you to His nature.

> But all of us who are Christians have no veils on our faces, but reflect like mirrors the glory of the Lord. We are transfigured by the Spirit of the Lord in ever-increasing splendour into his own image." II Cor 3:18, PHILLIPS.

> But we Christians have no veil over our faces; we can be mirrors that brightly reflect the glory of the Lord. And as the Spirit of the Lord works within us, we become more and more like him." II Cor 3:18, TLB

PARTAKING OF WORSHIP EXPERIENCE

Those who seek *only* what they might get from God's hands end up losing both the blessings of His Hands and joy of His presence. He wants you to primarily worship Him because when you do, the ensuing experiences produce every other thing that you need, including material blessings.

God lives in (inaccessible) light. This is the light of His glory which no one can see and yet be alive. Moses asked to be shown God's glory (Exodus 33:18) but God denied this request. See verse 20.

Dwelling In God's Secret Place

Even though you're not permitted to *see* God's glory and be alive, when you faithfully worship Him, the glory of His presence makes at least *four* things happen.

> Problems and ignorance are companions. When you remove the latter, the former disappears. You can only proffer solution to a problem that is known.

(i) *Divine Revelation.* The supernatural controls the natural. Every problem or solution first begins in the spirit realm of which most humans are ignorant.

Problems and ignorance are companions. When you remove the latter, the former disappears. You can only proffer solution to a problem that is known. When we have divine direction, we have enlightened (spiritual) mind. Then, mysteries are unveiled and hidden secrets of success and of victory are uncovered.

At a time when the apostles were "worshiping the Lord and fasting," the Holy Spirit gave them divine direction and said, "Set apart for me Barnabas and Saul for the work to which I have called them." Acts 13:2, NIV.

In Exodus 33: 9-10, cloudy pillars descended and stood at the door of the tabernacle and the

LORD talked with Moses. When the people saw this, they "rose up and worshipped..." What was the aftermath? God gave *direction* to Moses with a promise, "My presence shall go with thee, and will give thee rest." (v 14). In both instances where people worshiped God, they got divine revelation that gave direction.

(ii) *Divine Transformation.* Scripturally, transformation is a change in your spiritual form or nature. God is supernatural (Spirit). See John 4:23-24). You've got to connect with Him with your sanctified spirit. When God's glory settles on you, it produces an experience that quickens (animates) your spirit man which produces changes in your soul, and which ultimately changes the way you view things and the way you live.

Saul of Tarsus (later known as Paul) was on his way to persecute the followers of Jesus when "suddenly there shined round about him a light from heaven..." and Jesus began to speak to him. (Acts 9:1-22). That was an experience that birthed transformation. He became a witness to the Way. A bad guy turned to a godly, reformed man!

Jesus took Peter, James, and John to a mountain to pray, and He got transformed. "His appearance changed dramatically in their presence; and His face shone [with heavenly glory, clear and bright] like the sun, and His clothing became as white as light..." (Matt 17:2, AMP).

(iii) *Divine Wisdom.* Wisdom is the right application of knowledge and understanding. If you look at Proverbs 4, you'll see the excellency and supremacy of wisdom. Verse 7 says that wisdom is the principal thing. There's virtually nothing that God's family members can need on earth that God's wisdom can't provide. When God's Spirit of wisdom dwells in you, you'll not only prosper materially but also spiritually.

(iv) *Divine Joy.* God's glorious settling not only comes with wisdom but also with joy. *While happiness depends on happenstances which don't usually last long, Joy is an internal constant experience that is birthed and sustained by the person of God rather than largess of men.*

Joy is a fruit of the Holy Spirit. As such, it's an

> The glory left the Israelites' camp because the custodians of the ark substituted worship for profanity. The consequence was that the Israelites became vulnerable to their enemies. It's a vain thought to indulge in inequities and expect to be covered by God's glory!

experience of an overflowing life in God's house

where we have eternal pleasure. In Psalm 16:11, David said, "You make the path of life known to me. Complete joy is in your presence. Pleasures are by your side forever." (GW).

It's such an invaluable experience to behold God's glory that is ever present in His house. There's nothing else to desire in life that God's revelation, transformation, wisdom, and joy unlimited, cannot offer. No wonder then that David testified of God, "The boundary lines have fallen for me in pleasant places; surely I have a delightful inheritance." (Ps 16:6, NIV). Your inheritance is indeed blessed!

"SEE" GOD'S GLORY

In John 11:40 Jesus assured Martha that if she believed in God, she would "see the glory of God." Jesus prayed to God and then in a loud voice, called Lazarus back to life. And the dead man came out alive! God brought down the glory (the presence of God) through Jesus and created an experience of awe and wonders.

In Jesus, we see humility, holiness, orderliness, cleanliness, righteousness, forthrightness, working of miracles (doing the impossible) – raising the dead, instant healing, and restoration. As a member of God's family, you can experience these.

In both Exodus 33 and John11, Moses and Martha, Mary and the sympathizers did not "see God" physically but they experienced His glory which manifested His presence. Therefore, an experience of God's glory is both evidence of our covering and the manifestation of God's power that helps us to complete our respective assignments in this side of eternity.

DON'T MISTAKE SHADOW FOR DARKNESS

A shelter doesn't always indicate darkness.

Darkness is mostly associated with evils and typifies inequities. Devil and evil people represent darkness because of their evil works that can't withstand light.

When you are in God's family, you automatically become the devil's worst enemy. God lives in light and is full of light because He is the light. His presence is light and that's why you should never indulge in inequities because they would strip you of God's covering and make you vulnerable to the devil.

In I Samuel chapter 4, the Philistines captured the ark of the Lord's covenant. The Israelites moved the ark from the holiest of holy to the camp while the war was imminent (contrary to God's command that the ark should be in the holiest of holy place). To their amazement however, they lost the battles to the Philistines who captured the ark. In the process, Eli's two sons were dead.

Phinehas' wife who was then pregnant went into labor and gave birth to a baby named Ichabod, the Hebrew word that means "without glory." The mother had said, "the glory had departed from Israel" because of the capture of the ark and the death of her father-in-law and her husband. (1 Samuel 4:20-22).

Eli was unable to check his son's irreverent behaviors. His sons would take advantage of women worshippers and dispossess them of the sacrifices that were meant to be offered to give glory to God. Hophni and Phinehas had hijacked the sacrifices and worship items. And God was denied the glory thereof. God was angry. The ark was captured. The symbol of glory had departed.

The glory left the Israelites' camp because the custodians of the ark substituted worship for profanity. The consequence was that the Israelites became vulnerable to their enemies. It's a vain thought to indulge in inequities and expect to be covered by God's glory!

YOUR WORSHIP AND GOD'S GLORY

Your worship, which might include sacrifices (of praises and of material substances), are meant to give honor and glory to God. The glory of worship (meant for God alone) can be experienced when

Dwelling In God's Secret Place

we return to the Lord in repentance and begin to live in obedience.

The bottom line is this: Even though the shadow of the Almighty typifies His glory which is all-embracing and provides protective cover, it might not provide for your much needed covering until you make it your permanent abode.

> God's primary goal for bringing you into His family is to be conformed to His nature. Other things such as material blessings and healing are secondary!
>
> The settling of God's glory is more than a cloud, lightening, or smoke. His glory carries His Spirit, which is the number one catalyst for transformation.
>
> The Bible tells us that with open faces, we all behold the glory of the Lord and get "changed into the same image from glory to glory, even as by the Spirit of the Lord." (II Cor 3:18).
>
> God's Spirit will however transform you to the extent of your surrender, openness, and willingness.

Before we end this chapter, it's important to stress the fact that you should not mistake God's glory for glamor (physical allurements that can be counterfeited).

You may see many manifestations of *gifts* that dazzle people into different directions. These are not conclusive evidence of God's *glory*. Bad people can also make counterfeits. Demons do dazzle. Fake people can tantalize. There are fake prophets.

People often perform grandiose acts with ulterior, deceitful motives. The end does not always justify the means. God is interested in *how* as much as He is interested in *what* we do.

God is holy and inhabits holy dwelling.

SOMETHING TO THINK ABOUT

Reflection Point	The uniqueness of the shadow of the Almighty is shown in His glory. And His glory covers His *family members.* Are you one of them?
Scripture Focus	II Corinthians 3:18 - But all of us who are Christians have no veils on our faces, but reflect like mirrors the glory of the Lord. We are transfigured by the Spirit of the Lord in ever-increasing splendour into his own image." (PHILLIPS).

Note

_____
_____
_____
_____
_____
_____
_____

Segun Adepoju

6

The Great Covering

He shall cover thee with his feathers, and under his wings
shalt thou trust: his truth shall be thy shield and buckler. Psalm 91:4

O Jerusalem, Jerusalem, the city that kills the prophets
and stones God's messengers!
How often I have
wanted to gather
your children together
as a hen protects her
chicks beneath her wings,
but you wouldn't let me.
Luke 13:34, NLT

A cover or hiding place matters to most, if not all living beings.

This chapter discusses God's covering under three parts, as stated in Psalm 91:4 – (i) covering by feathers and wings, (ii) trusting in God's wings, and (iii) finding shield and buckler in God's truth.

I used to have a small garden where I planted tomatoes, pepper, spinach, and bitter leaf tree.

The 2022 summer came with severe weather conditions. It was unusually hot, even with a few rainfalls. The plants and flowers gave way to cracked grounds. Thanks to the sprinkler systems!

The bitter leaf tree had grown considerably with some leaves. When I noticed that the spinach, pepper, and tomatoes had fallen off despite constant watering, I did another planting, but this time, close to the grown tree, hoping that the impact of the scorching sun would be reduced. Yes, it worked, and they started growing.

The growth however became short-lived during the December 2022 winter blast. In three days, all the plants became withered. The garden partly looked like the plants were boiled. No thanks to the 16 degree Fahrenheit weather (which is very rare in my neighborhood).

(i) COVERING BY FEATHER AND WING

If you've seen a mother hen behave during or after hatching, or when danger lurks around her and the chicks, then you would understand the importance of feather and wing to winged animals. The mother eagle will never allow you to move near her eaglets, let alone kill them. They fight tooth and nail to protect their eggs or eaglets from external aggression.

SIMILITUDE OF HEN AND CHICKS

In Luke 13:34. Jesus said, "O Jerusalem, Jerusalem, the city that kills the prophets and stones God's messengers! How often I have wanted to gather your children together as a hen protects her chicks beneath her wings, but you wouldn't let me." (NLT).

How does hen protect her chicks?

First, the mother hen clucks, and the chicks understand that it's a call to take shelter because danger is looming. Then as chicks run toward her, she fluffs her feathered wings to create space for protection. At this stage, the hen becomes bigger.

Next, the mother hen spreads her tail which goes up, and this is followed by guttural sound (growling), more like sounding an alarm – warning to the predator and signal for chicks to take shelter in her expanded wings. At this stage, the hen looks dangerous, becomes aggressive and is ready to fight to protect the chicks.

> One of the signs of our maturity is the ability to hear and understand God's voice.

Feathered wings provide necessary warmth for the eggs during hatching, and even after, they provide protection from wintry weather. Aggressive winged animals (like eagles) have reportedly killed snakes and other dangerous animals who wanted to feast on their eggs and eaglets.

The use of feather and wings here in Luke 13:34 is a *simile* which compares how God would have loved to protect the Israelites if they had let Him.

Clucking of mother hen. This compares to God's voice calling us to come to Him for protection. In John 10, Jesus used metaphor to teach us that He is the good (true, authentic) shepherd; the sheep listen to His voice. He calls His own sheep by name and leads them out. (See John 10:1-16). God speaks to us in diverse ways including His written word (*logos*), revealed or inspired word (*rhema*), through angels, dreams, visions, and prophets.

One of the signs of our maturity is the ability to hear and understand God's voice. Through God's voice you know when the enemy of your soul (devil) is prowling and seeking to tear you apart.

It is wisdom to run to God for shelter!

Fluffing of feathered wings. The salvation room is elastic; it can take as many as they run there for cover. Jesus has already completed it by His blood. Mark 10:45 says that Jesus came to serve, and to give His life as a ransom for many. John 1:12 tells us that as many as received Him, to them He gave power (right) to become the sons of God, even to them that believe on His name.

One interesting thing to know is that the feather is warm inside. The Lord Almighty is big and inexorable as far as sustenance is concerned.

Growling. God's children are many and not everyone is the same. Some hear His voice once and obey while some will not, until danger looms. God is the omniscient; He can see and know many dangers around us of which we're oblivious. We should learn to be like David when He said, "God hath spoken once; twice have I heard this; that power belongeth unto God." (Ps 62:11).

Fighting in defense. God is ready to fight for us. He fought to liberate Israelites from their Egyptian overlord. He fought against Ai, Amalekites, Philistines, Assyrians, and a host of others, to ensure that the Israelites got to the promise land. Psalm 105:14 says God "suffered no man to do them wrong: yea, he reproved kings for their sakes." He also fought in defense of Moses, Abraham, David, Peter, Paul, and a host of other saints.

The world is full of evil and dangerous beings. Our salvation in Christ assures us of protections afforded by the blood of Jesus and the wonders of His name. As humans, we often get befuddled with different strokes of afflictions from difficulties of life.

Sometimes, our limitations and inequities repress us, and confine us to the ground where we become vulnerable to the snakes, pythons, and lions in the jungles of life. Indeed, our weaknesses draw us into dangers and inequities.

When we run to God, He covers us with His feathers, and we become invisible to our pursuers. When the battles confront us on the ground, His feathers cover us.

When the afflictions and battles rage in space, He's got the wings to move us higher. I like Michael W. Smith's song titled "Mighty to save." It tells of our victory in Jesus Christ. What can He not do? Romans 8:32 says, "He that spared not his own Son, but delivered him up for us all, how shall he not with him also freely give us all things?"

(ii) TRUSTING IN GOD'S WINGS

Psalm 91:4 says in part that, "under his wings shalt thou trust..." In chapter 4, we talked extensively about the "shadow of God's wings" under which David, Ruth, and Moses took cover.

In the Bible, God's acts of supernatural protection and deliverance are often associated with "God's wings." The Bible speaks of how God found Jacob (Israel) in the dangers of the wilderness and how he rescued him with his wings.

> He found him in a desert land, in the howling wasteland of a wilderness; He kept circling him, He took care of him, He protected him as the apple of His eye. "As an eagle that protects its nest, that flutters over its young, he spread out His wings and took them, He carried them on His pinions. Deut 32:10-11, AMP.

Pinion in a bird is the outer rear edge of the wing which contains its primary feathers (flight feathers). See further, Exodus 19:4.

Wings give protection and stability for flight. Their use is symbolic of protection reserved for

> Trust is a product of relationship; deeper trust is borne out of deeper relationship.

the family of God. But because it doesn't work like a magic, you must fear God to get the desired results and acknowledge Him as your succor.

In Malachi 4:2, God said, "But for you who fear My name [with awe-filled reverence] the sun of righteousness will rise with healing in its wings. And you will go forward and leap [joyfully] like calves [released] from the stall." (AMP). The "Sun of Righteousness" here was foretelling of Jesus Christ's power of healing. And the result would be great deliverance and escape from afflictions.

Trust and believing are often used interchangeably. It's one thing to have faith that God exists but it's another thing to trust in Him for a specific need or request. Most people have faith in God without trusting Him for certain things. Trust is a product of relationships; deeper trust is borne out of deeper relationships.

Someone who has never disappointed you before would earn a higher level of trust. Having faith in God means that you believe in Him (in his existence and power). Trusting in Him, however, means that you have confidence that He would do certain things for which you're trusting Him.

Dwelling in God's Secret Place

When you have confidence, you'd be bold and exude an attitude of conviction which shows in your action or inaction, speech, mannerism, and disposition. I mean, everyone around can tell when they see you.

Frankly, if you are a Christian, then, I assume that you know that God can do all things, but can you confidently demonstrate that you trust in God for performance of certain things you asked from him? Hebrews 4:16 admonishes us to come "boldly" before the throne of grace so we might obtain mercy and find grace in time of need.

> It's one thing to have faith that God exists but it's another thing to trust Him for a specific need or request.

Apostle Paul suffered greatly because of the gospel, yet he wasn't ashamed, based on the trust level and relationship he had with Jesus Christ. He said, "... for I know Him [and I am personally acquainted with Him] whom I have believed [with absolute trust and confidence in Him and in the truth of His deity], and I am persuaded [beyond any doubt] that He is able to guard that which I have entrusted to Him until that day [when I stand before Him]." (2 Tim 1:12, AMP).

(iii) TRUTH AS SHIELD AND BUCKLER

The last part of Psalm 91:4 says, "...his truth shall be thy shield and buckler."

John 8:31-32 tells us that if we abide by Jesus words (God's words) we're truly God' disciples and that we will know the truth and the truth will set us free.

In John 14:6, Jesus categorically states that He's the Way, the Truth, and the Life. In Titus 1:1, we learn that the knowledge of the truth leads to godliness. God's Word is the *truth*, and the *truth* is Jesus Christ. See John 1:1.

A shield is a protective equipment from external aggression. It is usually fastened to prevent penetration of enemies' arrows. A buckler is a protective cover object held by hand. Roman soldiers used to hold buckler in one hand and the sword with the other. This gave them a balance such that they could thrust (offend) with sword with one hand while defending with buckler with the other.

Ephesians 6:16 says you should take up the shield of faith with which you can extinguish the fiery darts (flaming arrows) of the evil one. And verse 17 says the sword of the Spirit is the word of God. From God's word you grow your faith to produce the shield to defend. Your faith in God and His word is your shield. And the same word can offend, like a buckler, when you know (through maturity) how to use it.

A practical way is to target a particular area in your life with certain *logos*, study them, confess and work them until they produce a *rhema* with which you fight the devil.

You must be sure that you are *in the truth* if you want the *truth* to be a defense and a weapon for you.

SUMMING IT UP

Recall the story about my garden that I shared earlier in this chapter. Let me briefly share three basic lessons I learned from it.

First, I planted the garden with some expectations.

We are like plants in God's Garden. Psalm 92:13 says that those who are planted in the house of the LORD shall flourish in the courts of our God. That's not all. Verse 14 says that they shall bear fruits in old age and shall be fresh and flourishing.

Why should you continue to bear fruit in old age? It's because in verse 15, Moses said, "*He is* my rock, and *there is* no unrighteousness in Him." (NKJV).

Second, to realize those expectations, I looked for a cover to preserve the plants from excessive heat.

God has certain expectations on us when He made us. He wanted us to flourish and be fruitful. In our salvation is our cover. We are the plants and God is the cover. Psalm 84:11 says that the Lord God is a sun and shield. And Psalm 30:5 says that God is a shield to those who take refuge in Him.

Third, the plants suffered from one extreme weather condition to another and as a result, both the cover and plants collapsed. The cover was limited in every sense of the word.

The categories of life extremities are never close. Whether we realize it or not, we're all troubled by life extremities at various times. But our survival or safety depends on who or what we run to, as cover. We have an unlimited cover in God.

Psalm 91:4 gives you access to the supernatural weapons that are available in the arsenal of God when you *dwell in God's secret place.*

> In our salvation is our cover. We are the plants and God is the cover.

Jesus fought and won the devil with the truth – the word of God. He confronted every temptation with "it is written…" He recollected and used the truth of God's word stated in Deuteronomy to fight and win battles in Matthew chapter 4. God's word is never stale. You just have to master its usage.

SOMETHING TO THINK ABOUT

Reflection Point	A chick that ignores the clucking and growling of the mother hen is in danger of predator. A dog that is doomed to get lost would abandon the guiding whistling of its owner. Jesus said that His sheep would hear His voice. Submitting to God's loving arms is the first step to enjoying the covering available in His house.
Scripture of the Day	John 10:27-28 - My sheep know my voice, and I know them. They follow me, and I give them eternal life, so that they will never be lost. No one can snatch them out of my hand. (CEV).

Note
_____
_____

Segun Adepoju

Part Three

From Fear to Life

===================

Your vision

and

your future

are intricately woven together.

If the devil can dim your vision

with fear, then, he has gotten hold of your future.

Whoever has destroyed your vision has potentially destroyed

you. John 10:10 says that devil comes to steal, kill, and destroy.

One of the ways he achieves this is by stealing your vision. He also achieves

this by filling your mind with barren ideas, and substitute eagles' eyes with chickens' eyes.

===================

7

Freedom From Fear (Pt. 1) (Weapon of Fear)

For God did not give us a spirit of
timidity *or* cowardice *or* fear,
but [He has given us a spirit] of power and
of love and of sound judgment *and* personal
discipline [abilities that result in a calm,
well-balanced mind and
self-control]. 2 Timothy 1:7, AMP.

Fear naturally emanates from
a confused mind because
confusions, uncertainties and
fears are companions.[3]

Psalm 91: 5-8 says:

Thou shalt not be afraid for the terror by night; nor for the arrow that flieth by day; Nor for the pestilence that walketh in darkness; nor for the destruction that wasteth at noonday. A thousand shall fall at thy side, and ten thousand at thy right hand; but it shall not come nigh thee. Only with thine eyes shalt thou behold and see the reward of the wicked.

Have you wondered why Moses had to allay our fears first?

The first weapon of the devil is fear, and it comes with great torment. Once you become a victim of fear, you lose your soul, spirit, and body to whatever comes with it.

THE WEAPON OF FEAR

It is neither the seasons nor the weather that cause dangers to mankind but what accompanies them. More specifically, it is not the summer but the accompanying excessive heat that causes harm to lives and properties. It is neither the fall nor the winter but accompanying excessive rains and tornadoes that cause destruction. Likewise, it's what comes with fear and how you respond that bring the catastrophes described in Psalm 91:5-8.

> ... it's what comes with fear and how you respond that bring the catastrophes described in Psalm 91:5-8.

In I kings 19, Elijah fled at the threat of Jezebel who had wanted to kill him. He was a fugitive of fear. Whereas In II Chronicles 32, Hezekiah stood his ground in the face of Sennacherib's threats against Jerusalem. Sennacherib, the King of Assyria, had threatened Judah whose inhabitants were already feeling the heat of the siege.

Hezekiah's (the King of Judah's) first line of actions was the deployment of large soldiers. And the first charge was against fear – "Be strong and courageous, be not afraid nor dismayed for the king of Assyria, nor for all the multitude that is with him: for there be more with us than with him." (v 7). The efficacy of this charge was calmness in the military formations. Verse 8 says, "...And the people rested themselves upon the words of Hezekiah king of Judah."

It was as if Hezekiah knew that Sennacherib's first weapon would be fear. The King of Assyrians' officers were deliberate in ensuring that all the inhabitants heard the Assyrians intimidation by threatening the people of Jerusalem in Hebrews (Jews) language. Verse 18 says that Sennacherib's officers "... cried with a loud voice in the Jews' speech unto the people of Jerusalem that were on the wall, to affright them, and to trouble them; that they might take the city." Then Hezekiah took the right and the best action. With prophet Isaiah, he prayed to God and God sent an angel who destroyed the Assyrians and saved Hezekiah. (Verses 20-23).

> Dare your fears with God's word.

David said in Psalm 56:3 that he would trust in God when he's afraid. Psalm 91:5 and 2 Chronicles 32:7 & 18 teach us that fear is a satanic device to first unsettle you. When he succeeds with this, as stated in John 10:10, he steals, kills, and destroys. That's why, like King Hezekiah, you must immediately *arrest* the spirit of fear in your heart (and in the hearts of your fellow "family members," encouraging them to stand first against Satan's antics.

God's word is life giving, quickening (John 6:63), and generates spiritual detoxification that neutralizes the impacts of fear. The renewed enthusiasm jolts you into a supernatural level of faith in God that makes you superior to the antics of the devil. It impacts your spirit and soul with unmatched dynamics and strategies to get past the limits placed before you by fears.

Dare your fears with God's word. A victory over fear is a victory over what comes with it. Fear has no place where God's word reigns.

FEAR DIMS YOUR VISION

A vision is an unfolding of a future. It is having a revelation, a mental picture or knowledge of the future before it arrives. As a member of God's family, there's a purpose for you in this side of eternity. God births (*downloads*) that purpose in your heart by His Spirit. And when you take hold of that purpose, you *catch the vision* and begin to execute it.

In God's kingdom, every believer has a unique purpose. It's up to you to *discover* and *execute* it. The

> A victory over fear is a victory over what comes with it.

earlier you do this, the better. Every other plan, dream and aspiration should *follow* your vision. In I Chronicles 22:7, David told his son Solomon that he (David) "intended to build a house" for the name of the Lord. Whereas this wasn't God's plan for him because he had shed a lot of blood.

Whether individually or corporately, nationally, or municipally, you can easily read and predict the absence of visions. All you have is disorderliness, fruitlessness, and barren regrets. *When nothing is conceived nothing will be achieved!* Proverbs 29:18 tells us that where there is no vision, the people perish. Another translation puts it this way: "If people can't see what God is doing, they stumble all over themselves; But when they attend to what he reveals, they are most blessed." (AMP).

In Numbers chapter 21, the Israelites had settled in the land of the Amorites but soon encountered oppositions from Og, the king of Bashan and his armies. Fear set in. But the first encouragement from God to Moses was to tell the Israelites not to be afraid of Og. If fear of Og had been able to dim Moses's eyes of promise land, then the results would have been devastating!

When God gives you a vision, he equips you with means of getting it actualized ("*provision*") which includes courage and faith to pursue it. In Ezra 3, the post-exilic returnees were set to rebuild the broken altar in Jerusalem. The vision was clear, and they prepared to execute it. But they were faced with fear of the enemies. Ezra 3:3 said that despite their fear of the opposition, they built the altar. In Ezra 4, there came another round of opposition to rebuild. The enemies of Judah resorted to deception and volunteered helping hands which were rejected.

According to Ezra 4:4, the peoples around the returnees *set to discourage* and make them afraid to go on building by hiring *counselors* to work against the people of Judah and to frustrate their plans. Even though the project was halted for some time, God put wisdom in the hearts of the leaders of Judah. By King's Darius' fiat, the project was completed and dedicated.

> Fear has no place where God's word reigns.

God's wisdom is manifold. He will raise help against the fear of the enemies. This may come by ways of unusual faith, unusual wisdom, uncommon courage, or ways that are unfathomable. By any means, never give in to fear!

GOD'S FEATHER IS THICKER THAN FEAR

If you are covered by God's feathers and find refuge in His wings as you trust in Him, and if His truth (word) becomes your weapons, then you have nothing to fear. You would openly declare like David in Psalm 27:1-3, "The Lord is my light and my salvation; he protects me from danger—whom shall I fear…?" (TLB).

The evils that can come against one in life are manifold. They come in sizes, phases, and stages. And when they visit, they come with fear. They include "terror by night," "arrow that flieth by day," "pestilence that walketh in darkness," and "destruction that wasteth at noonday" (collectively let us term them as "misfortunes" or "catastrophes") which may ultimately result in death. The calming assurance is that they shall not come near you because of God's abiding presence.

David was a veteran shepherd who used some of his learning experiences to write Psalm 23. He understood how sheep would run to him for safety in the event of dangers or deadly weather conditions. David confidently wrote, "The Lord is my shepherd ... though I walk through the valley of the shadow of death, I will fear no evil: for thou art with me..." (Ps 23:1 & 4). God is the head of the family and would not let misfortunes befall any member of the family, including you.

It is easier for Moses to say that God will protect you from all types of misfortunes and that would be fine. But when he said that you shall

> When nothing is conceived, nothing will be achieved!

"not be afraid" of these misfortunes, he wanted to show more than mere protections. He wanted to emphasize the need for members of God's family to understand that, among other things, *fear is the gateway to bondage. And once fear is dealt with, whatever comes with it, is inconsequential.*

Jesus' disciples were overcome with fear of tempest and ran to Him for help, saying "Lord, save us! We are perishing!" His first line of solution was a question to them, "Why are you fearful, O you of little faith?" See Mathew 8:23-27. Jesus did not calm the tempest first but instead, addressed their fear. Hebrews 5:14-15 tells us that Jesus came that "... he might destroy him that had the power of death, that is, the devil;

And deliver them who through fear of death were all their lifetime subject to bondage."

When your heart seems soaked in your boiling blood, running helter-skelter without first addressing the fear first would create more troubles. Fears and solutions are never friends. So, fear not, the master Jesus is in the boat with you.

> Fear is more than emotions; it is an evil spirit. It subjects people to sickness, bondage, and death.

NIGHT AND DAY – 24/7 PROTECTION

Night and day, as used in Psalm 91:5, connotes twenty-four hours cycle. Starting from 6pm, night begins and ends at 5:59am when a day begins. In John 11:19, Jesus said, "Are there not twelve hours in the day..." While the sentence might connote making opportunities count, especially while we're agile, the fact remains that twelve hours of night and twelve hours of day represent twenty-four hours cycle.

Whether the misfortunes happen in the day or at night, it does not matter because the efficacy of God's words is 24/7. Hallelujah!

Dwelling in God's Secret Place

SOMETHING TO THINK ABOUT

Reflection Point	Fears grow from the seeds that the devil sows (in your heart). Faith grows from the seed of God's word. You grow, enjoy your life, or become mature, according to the measure of your freedom over fear. Fears and solutions are never friends!
Scriptures of the Day	**II Timothy 1:7** – "For God did not give us a spirit of timidity *or* cowardice *or* fear, but [He has given us a spirit] of power and of love and of sound judgment *and* personal discipline [abilities that result in a calm, well-balanced mind and self-control]. (AMP). **Romans 8:15** – "For the Spirit that God has given you does not make you slaves and cause you to be afraid; instead, the Spirit makes you God's children, and by the Spirit's power we cry out to God, "Father! my Father!" (GNT).

Note

_____
_____
_____
_____
_____

Segun Adepoju

8

Freedom From Fear (Pt. 2) (Scriptural Panacea for Overcoming Fear)

Fear not: for I have
redeemed thee, I have called
thee by thy name; thou art mine. Is 43:1

The LORD is my light and my salvation;
I will fear no one. The LORD protects me
from all danger; I will never be afraid. When evil
people attack me and try to kill me, they stumble and
fall.
Even if a whole army surrounds me, I will not be
afraid;
even if enemies attack me, I will still trust God. Ps
27:1-3, GNT

Do not be afraid *and* anxious, little flock,
for it is your Father's good pleasure to give you the
kingdom. Lk 12;32, AMP

And he said, Fear not, for they that are with us are
more than they that are with them. 2 Kg 6:16,
DARBY.

I have never seen or heard of anyone who never fears. The difference, however, ranges from what we fear, our attitudes to fear and whom we run to when fear grips us.

Let me illustrate this with a story of Anthony Evans' niece, Kariss, as shared by Anthony[4] in the book titled *Divine Disruption*.[5]

> A little girl by the name of Karris was playing on the sidewalk and a big German dog made his way toward her and started barking and baring his teeth. She screamed and ran toward her grandfather, Dr. Tony Evans who grabbed her and wrapped her around his arms. For a while, Karris was sobbing but after a while she looked up to her grandpa and then looked down at the dog and then stopped crying.
>
> Guess what Karris did when she got her confidence back in her grandpa's arms. She started taunting the dog, "Nanny, nanny, boo-boo." In Anthony's words, "The circumstances did not change, but her perspective did. She was safe in the arms of her grandfather."

Categories of fear are never closed. We have fear of failure, of success (how to manage success), unknown, past (poor choices), other's opinions, mistakes, changes, sickness, diagnoses, sudden evils. We even have fear of space, height, water, sleep, etc. The peak of fear (which is common to all living beings) is that of death.

So then, the question is not whether you'll ever have fears but what you'll do when they come.

The point of emphasis in Karris' story is that *fear no longer has mastery over you when you realize that you're covered by trusted arms that are more powerful than your fear.* Even though the dog was still barking, Karris wasn't fearful again because of her confidence in the arms of his caring grandfather.

This reminds me of the hymn attributed to P. P. Bliss (1871) titled *"I am so glad that our father in Heaven."* The hymn's second stanza says,

> Though I forget Him and wander away,
> Kindly He follows whenever I stray;
> Back to His dear loving arms would I flee,
> When I remember that Jesus loves me.[6]

OVERCOMING FEAR

Let's discuss some scripturally sound ways you can overcome any type of fear.

(i)   *Trusting in the Lord.*

Trusting in the Lord is an expression of confidence that He would do what you asked of Him. Trust is borne out of experiences and relationships. If somebody never let you down before, then the chance of reposing your trust in the person would be higher.

In Ps 56:3, David told God, "When I am afraid, I will put my trust *and* faith in You." (AMP). As a background, David prayed this prayer when he fled from King Saul who wanted to kill him.

In I Samuel chapter 21, in apparent desperation, David went to Achish, the king of Gath (Gath is a Philistine territory) but he was found out, and the servants of the king recognized him as David. He was hurt because the place he had anticipated to be a good hideout turned out to be unsafe. He was then carrying multiple fears – fear of king Saul, fear of Achish, the king of Gath, fear of being apprehended and being handed over to Saul, and fear of identity as he pretended to be insane. (See I Samuel 21:10-13).

> "When I am afraid, I will put my trust and faith in You."

David's experiences that produced Psalm 56 came at a low period in his life where the easiest thing for him was to quit and surrender to king Saul, his archenemy. But not David! He knew of one person who could not disappoint in the face of fear.

David's ordeals stretched him to think past any form of human trust — in phantom "Goliath's sword" given to him earlier by Priest Abimelech, in Achish, king of Gath, in personal military experiences. That was a moment when bloody civilians cheaply molested the giant killer. He however trusted in God for deliverance. His faith and *trust* in God worked. He escaped to the cave of Adullam. (I Samuel 22:1).

Have you been through David's experiences highlighted above and felt like a candle near the flame of fire? Scary doctor's report? Protracted illness? Fear of looming business failure? Has money failed you before? Have trusted friends failed you before? Has your trust in your personal intelligence failed you before? Whatever it might be, put your trust, confidence, and faith in God. Psalm 125:1 says that those who trust in the LORD shall be as mount Zion, which cannot be removed, but abides forever.

(ii)   Remember the Lord first.

Most times fear grips your heart like a heart attack which doesn't give its victim the room to bid your neighbor farewell. Because fear takes over every part of you — spirit, soul, and body — many people spontaneously act out of fear before they realize it's too late to back out. But when fear strikes and you *remember the Lord* first, he'll quieten your spirit man and then your soul and body will feel the impulse and act under God's inspiration.

"Remembering the Lord" here is not about commemoration and is not an observance of certain festivals. It's more than "annual harvest thanksgiving". It's reflecting on the abilities of God displayed in the past and acknowledging His possibilities for the future in settled faith that's anchored on His promises. To remember is to open a memory about a person or thing. It is a state of your memory where you call certain things to mind. That implies that something was there before.

> "Remembering the Lord" here is ... not an observance of certain festivals. It's more than "annual harvest thanksgiving."

Sometimes we choose what we remember. At other times, remembering (or not remembering) past events is out of our control. This is where being a member of God's family is important. His (Holy) Spirit in us reminds us of God's promises, power to perform, and possibilities that abound in our inheritances in the saints. You remember how God helped in similar situations in the past. You remember His covenants and His ability to fulfil them. At this level, fear and doubts disappear. Faith (in God) develops (through our knowledge and understanding of His promises). The reward is that you're certain to know what to do.

Thankfully, we have the Holy Spirit as our *parakletos!*

(iii)   Walking in the reality of freedom by God's Spirit

2 Corinthians 3:17 says, "Now the Lord is that Spirit: and where the Spirit of the Lord is, there is liberty." We know that the Holy Spirit is our helper but we don't always walk in that reality. We are not conscious of Him. We put Him off. We fail to acknowledge Him and often break communication channels with Him. And so, when we face fears, we're left empty to battle fear; we're helpless.

We must walk and work with the Holy Spirit in order to experience the reality of our freedom in Christ Jesus.

(iv)   Seeking the Lord

When you seek, you heartily and intentionally make efforts to find (someone) who is knowingly in existence. The connotation is that you're sure that finding the object (or the person) will result in certain benefits to you. Seeking takes effort, resources, and may take time. Sometimes pain goes with seeking.

In Psalm 34:4, David said, "I sought the LORD, and he heard me, and delivered me from all my fears." Remember all the shades of fear that befell David in I Samuel 21. Then he trusted in God in the face of probable arrest and deportation to King Saul's territory. In the process, he pretended to be insane and king Achish of Gath sent him away (it was the tradition to not harm mentally deranged people).

Recall that David lied to priest Abimelech earlier in Chapter 21 that he was on an urgent errand for king Saul. He later got to his wit's end. Then he testified in Psalm 34 that he sought the Lord who heard and delivered him from all his fears. Here, David had weighed all options and concluded that seeking God is the best route when faced with sundry fears.

How then do you *seek* God?

The rest of the verses in Psalm 34 gives us the clue.

(a) *Looking unto Him*. You must direct your expectations toward Him. Looking unto God connotes acknowledging Him and focusing on Him as the source of your needs, including protection and material blessings. He may then choose to use anyone and anything to answer your prayers – friends, family members, animals, etc. God used raven to feed Elijah. He used fish to swallow and vomit Jonah so that he could preach repentance to the wayward Nineveh. Psalm 34: 5 says those who look unto Him are never covered with shame.

(b) *Calling unto God in prayers.* Verse 6 says, "this poor man called, and the Lord heard him; saved him out of all his troubles" (NIV). Calling unto God could mean praying to Him. Prayer is a way of showing your dependence on Him. David was helpless, poor, fearful, in tight spot, and in a state of uncertainty when he prayed to God, and he was heard. No matter how blessed you are, prayers are never enough. Even Jesus prayed until point of death. Keep seeking God in prayers. (See I Thessalonians 5:17; Luke 18:1; Matthew 7:7-8).

(c) *Fearing the Lord.* In this context, *fearing* God implies reverencing and honoring Him. It means you are abstaining from wickedness not necessarily because of attendant punishment but due to your love for God. Fearing God means hating what He hates and loving what He loves.

Psalm 34:7 says that the angel of the Lord surrounds those who *fear* the Lord and delivers them. Verse 9 is compelling: "O [reverently] fear the LORD, you His saints (believers, holy ones); For to those who fear Him there is no want." (AMP).

Lions are the kings of the jungle, very powerful enough to secure their daily needs. With all their abilities, they still suffer hunger and many of them have died of hunger. In your case, your provider is God, and your safety depends on Him.

Once you *seek* God in holy fear in all your dealings, He'll meet your needs. According to verse 10, "The young lions lack [food] and grow hungry, But they who seek the LORD will not lack any good thing." (AMP).

David refused to kill King Saul because he feared God. No wonder God in turn delivered him from his fears! Joseph feared God and refused to sleep with Potiphar's wife, even though no one might have probably found out. You fear God when you should have taken revenge for an offence, but you didn't.

(d)   *Keeping tongues from evil.* Under Psalm 34:12-13, to have a full life and see many good days, you must keep your tongue from evil and your lips from telling lies.

Have you noticed that in almost all situations, your first reaction when faced with fearful situations is negative utterances? "I know the scan result is gonna be bad..." Or "God, where were you when all of these happened to me?" Or, as Naomi said, "... Call me not Naomi, call me Mara: for the Almighty hath dealt very bitterly with me." (Ruth 1:20).

Naomi was very shortsighted. Otherwise, she would have realized that God is the master architect of life; He can design and redesign, shape and reshape, make, and unmake any life events to glorify Himself in our situations. The fact that Jesus Christ hailed from the lineage started by the union of Boaz and Ruth proved Naomi wrong.

> One of the ways to discern a wise man from a fool is his utterances.

James 3:2 says, "... If anyone does not stumble in what he says [never saying the wrong thing], he is a perfect man [fully developed in character, without serious flaws], able to bridle his whole body *and* rein in his entire nature [taming his human faults and weaknesses]." (AMP).

Your maturity, character, and integrity are intricately connected to the quality of your life. *One of the ways to discern a wise man from a fool is his utterances.* The result is often bad when he's in a difficult life condition. Guard your life by guarding your tongue.

(e) *Turn away from evil.* Seeking God and embracing evils are diametrically opposite. You must choose one.

When devil overwhelms your life with heavy storms as he did to Job, Lazarus, and his family, and as in Nain's widow's case, the easy click is to resort to evils such as retaliation, unforgiveness, crimes and related vices. These are what fears can drive one into. These are broader roads, and many people find their ways there.

You must however try to pause for a moment and then turn to God, seek Him in holy fear, love, and reverence (worship). Psalm 34:14 says, "Depart from evil, and do good; seek peace, and pursue it."

Finally, I want to conclude that it's important for you to treat fear as your enemy. It disturbs your soul and springs up anxieties which move you in the direction of wrong choices which might make you disobey God.

At a time during his reign, King Saul was overcome with fear. His troops were "quaking with fear" and he lost his patience and went ahead to offer sacrifices (which he wasn't meant to offer).

Prophet Samuel challenged him. Look at Saul's excuse, "… 'I thought… and I have not sought the Lord's favor.' So I felt compelled to offer the burn offering." (I Samuel 13:12, NIV). Fear birthed anxieties which moved King Saul and the armies against God's will. Fear prevented him from seeking the Lord first.

John Newton's hymn, *Begone, Unbelief*[7] is very useful here. The first and fourth stanzas read:

> Begone, Unbelief,
> My Savior is near,
> And for my relief
> Will surely appear;
> By prayer let me wrestle,
> And He will perform;
> With Christ in the vessel,
> I smile at the storm.

> Since all that I meet
> Shall work for my good,
> The bitter is sweet,
> The medicine, food;
> Though painful at present,
> 'Twill cease before long,
> And then, oh, how pleasant
> The conqueror's song!

It's chilling to know that you have as your shield, the Almighty God who is unlimited in every way! His loving arms are too tender to reject. His invisible hands are too strong and righteous to fail to grasp you in distress. His glorious presence is too secured to expose you to the enemy. He is the unlimited, infinite, inscrutable God.

The past and the future are no barriers to God because, to Him, your past and your future are as clear as the present. He doesn't have past, and He can't have a future because, He was before the past, and He will ever be ahead of time and space. After Him is Him. He sees everywhere as clear as His palm.

In fact, you are likened to Jerusalem, His beloved city, and as He had assured, "See, I have inscribed you on the palms of My hands; Your walls are continually before Me." (Is 49:16, NKJV).

As a dweller in God's secret place who trusts in God's safe arms, you don't need to be afraid of the misfortunes of any type even though they continue to rage. You must shift your attention and perspectives to God, the master of the universe, the Emperor and King – the Head of the Family.

Dwelling in God's Secret Place

SOMETHING TO THINK ABOUT

Reflection Point	Don't allow fear to tear your life down with what you say. There is a connection between your tongue and your life, anatomically, physiologically, and psychologically.
Scripture Focus	**Romans 8:15** – "For the Spirit that God has given you does not make you slaves and cause you to be afraid; instead, the Spirit makes you God's children, and by the Spirit's power we cry out to God, "Father! my Father!" (GNT).

Note

_____
_____
_____
_____
_____
_____
_____

9

The Great Deliverance and Protection by God's Angels

Surely He shall deliver thee from
the snare of the fowler, and from the noisome
pestilence. Psalm 91:3

For He will command His angels in regard to you, To
protect *and* defend
and guard you in all your ways [of obedience and
service]. Ps 91:11, AMP

But for twenty-one days the mighty Evil Spirit who
overrules the kingdom of Persia
blocked my way. Then Michael, one of the top officers
of the heavenly army, came to help me,
so that I was able to break through these spirit rulers
of Persia. Dan 10:13, TLB

Then war broke out in heaven. Michael and his angels
fought against the dragon, and the
dragon and his angels fought back. But he was not
strong enough, and they lost their place in heaven. Rev
12:7-8, NIV

For Moses, the certainty of God's deliverance is assured, having trusted in the Lord, his God. Hence the word, "surely" in verse 3.

SNARE OF THE FOWLER

The use of snare of the fowler in Psalm 91:3 is a metaphor.

A fowler is a fowl (bird) catcher. As used here, the Hebrew word *moqesh* means a snare which is a trap set to capture or destroy an object. Usually, a fowler puts baits on the trap to lure and ensnare birds. Fowler's snare here connotes traps of the devil and his agents.

Devil is the fowler - Here, the devil is the fowler who seeks to trap God's children by luring (tempting) them into doing what God hates. For example, after many failed attempts by Balaam (who was employed by Balak, King of Moab) to curse the Israelites, Balaam counseled Balak to seduce the Israelites to sin against God. He knew that this would make God turn against the Israelites. And that's what happened!

> ... the Hebrew word *moqesh* means a snare which is a trap set to capture or destroy an object.

According to Numbers 25:1-3 the Israelites fell for prostitution and idolatry (worshipping of Baal of Peor). Of course, God was angry with them. The consequences were unpleasant. See Numbers 25:1-8; 1 Corinthians 10:1-13.

John 10:10 describes the devil as a thief which comes to steal, kill, and destroy. 1 Peter 5:8 instructs us to be self-controlled and alert because the devil, our enemy, like a roaring lion, prowls around like a lion, looking for whom to devour.

The devil doesn't pose as a fearful image in dirty rags with horns on his head and with rolling, bulging eyes. He can use anybody as his agents including friends, family members, mentors, leaders, pastors, and colleagues. Wicked people are found everywhere, even among "God's people." The Bible tells us that "... wicked men are found among my people, they watch like fowlers who lie in wait; they set a trap, they catch men." (Jere 5:26, AMP).

I want to suggest to you to arm yourself with the mentality that anybody can be devil's agent and you will be careful to exercise control in your relationships.

The snare is the temptation – The devil's snare is his trap which is the temptation. The bait is sin. If you bite the bait, then you've fallen into his temptation. Do not make mistakes about it. He likes to coat sins with pleasant look, funny sound, enticing smell, and with attraction that appeals to human sensual desires such that many are already in his trap before they realize their waywardness.

The trap may begin as a little quarrel that grows into malice and unforgiveness. In Numbers 25 quoted above, the snare was sin (of prostitution and idolatry).

Devil's bait is basically sin but may manifest in anger, jealousy, unforgiveness, malice, idolatry, fear, and a host of works of the flesh. But you have the highest assurance of protection from God who has promised to deliver you from the devil's trap.

In teaching the disciples how to pray, Jesus said, "Lead us not into temptation." (Luke 11:4). So, if you have fallen for it already, then, ask God for forgiveness and deliverance. If you are yet to, then, pray not to fall into it.

> The devil's snare is his trap which is the temptation. The bait is sin. Don't fall into it.

NOISOME PESTILENCE

Pestilence is a deadly epidemy. Its Hebrew word *havvah* means rushing calamity from which everything gives way. Noisome pestilence is worse. It is when calamity is accompanied by destructive noises. Hurricanes such as Katrina and Harvey are close examples of noisome pestilence. They come with fury, noises, and catastrophes.

As used in Psalm 91, noisome pestilence might not necessarily be sweeping, destructive natural disasters. It represents any type of misfortunes that can befall men. Covid-19 pandemic that wiped off many businesses, plagued, and killed millions of people was destructive enough to fall under this category. It caused havoc but it doesn't mean that God didn't know about it. May such never happen again.

There were people dear to us that went with Covid-19. It came with many sorrows but at the same time, it left survivors.

In everything, the Bible says we should give thanks. Here is the testimony. Even though many went with it, if they were God's family members, then, all hope isn't lost. They will live with God eternally.

PROTECTION BY GOD'S ANGELS

Psalm 91:11-12 says, "For he shall give his angels charge over thee, to keep thee in all thy ways. They shall bear thee up in their hands, lest thou dash thy foot against a stone."

Angels are God's special messengers or ministering spirits. They may however appear in human form. They don't act anyhow on their own but on specific requests of God or of His children. Thus, their ministry isn't just for anybody but to those who merit it. The merit requirements include calling them for a just cause, being a born again child of God and abiding in God's secret place, living in obedience to God's instructions, and fearing Him.

When Jesus was betrayed by Judas Iscariot and was about to be arrested by armed men, one of Jesus' loyalists, in defense, cut off one of the men's ears. Jesus told His loyalist to put back his sword and said, "Do you think I cannot call on my Father, and he will at once put at my disposal more than twelve legions of angels?" (Matt 26:53, NIV).

> Angels are God's special messengers or ministering spirits.

Twelve legions of angels approximately totaled eighty thousand angels. He came for a just cause. So, God would have approved the dispatch. Hebrews 1:14 calls angels "ministering spirits sent to serve those who will inherit salvation." Psalm 34:7 tells us that the angel of the LORD is a guard; he surrounds and defends all who fear Him. (NLT).

God can protect you through His angels in any way, by any means, and anywhere.

Giving His Angels Charge Over You

Why would God "give His angels charge" over you and why would He trust angels that much? First, He created all things including the angels. Besides, He is the one who commissions and empowers them.

Moreover, God created angels for errands for the benefits of members of His family. That is why they are powerful beings. At a time in Israelites' history, they were under Assyrian bondage. But when God was ready to deliver them, He sent an angel.

2 Kings 19:35 tells us that in one night, the angel of God went out and put to death a hundred and eighty-five thousand men in Assyrian camp. So, if one angel could eliminate thousands of people, then, I wonder how many who revolt against you that God's angels (notice the plural form) can't defeat.

To keep Thee in All Thy Ways

Psalm 74:20 tells us that dark places of the earth are full of the habitations of cruelty. As humans, we are finite and limited by many things, especially the things that are beyond our understanding. Our ignorance thus seems to be the devil's breeding ground. But we don't have to know everything because we know the God who knows everything.

We're not alone! Whether the dangers are physical or spiritual, God's angels can keep us from them. That's why God's angels will keep us "in all our ways."

Notice that when devil tempted Jesus in Matthew 4:6 he omitted "in all thy ways." Devil was mischievous, knowing that "in all thy ways" made a lot of difference. "In all thy ways" describes every type of situation you can find yourself – temptation, fowler's snare, sorrow, joy, and good mood, in your job or at home. This assurance makes a big difference.

Lest Thou Dash Thy Foot Against a Stone

Angels bearing you up in their hands and preventing you from dashing your foot against a stone are metaphors. Bearing you up in His hands means a supernatural lifting from dangers. "Stone" here connotes dangers and hardness of life.

I want to say that the Angels have the powers to do all of these for you physically or supernaturally because they are mighty creatures. Angels have reportedly rescued people from accidents.

God's angels can guide, guard, instruct, encourage, comfort, and deliver good news. See Luke 2:9, 15; 1 Chronicles 21:18; Mathew 4:11.

> God's purpose for sending His angels to keep you in all your ways is for the fulfilment of His purpose(s) for your life. Even if you are not a member of God's house and you enjoy angels' ministry, this kindness is to protect God's stake in your life with a view to having you saved from the greater and eternal death.
>
> Angels can't be used like robots, charms, or money. Their exploits relate to destiny fulfilment and not to protect frivolities, immorality, or crimes.
>
> God's angels are messengers and should not be worshipped. See Colossians 2:18. Only God is to be worshipped. See Hebrews 1:6; Revelation 4:8-9; 5:8-14; Exodus 34:14; Deuteronomy 6:13-14 & Matthew 4:10.

Finally, let me conclude on the note of Fanny Crosby's hymn, *"He Hideth My Soul[8]."* Stanzas one and two read:

> A wonderful Savior is Jesus my Lord,
> A wonderful Savior to me.
> He hideth my soul in the cleft of the rock
> Where rivers of pleasure I see.

Refrain:
He hideth my soul in the cleft of the rock
That shadows a dry, thirsty land.
He hideth my life in the depths of his love,
And covers me there with his hand,
And covers me there with his hand.

A wonderful Savior is Jesus my Lord;
He taketh my burden away.
He holdeth me up, and I shall not be moved;
He giveth me strength as my day.
(Refrain)

God's great hands (of deliverance and protection) are stronger than covid-19, cancer, pneumonia, barrenness, or any spirit behind the afflictions that might buffet you!

SOMETHING TO THINK ABOUT

Reflection Point	The bait that you know to be poison and the snare that you know to be dangerous can generally not kill you. With the help of the Holy Spirit, you can discern and know the fowler's snare and escape it.
Scripture Focus	Psalm 34:7 – "The angel of the LORD is a guard; he surrounds and defends all who fear him." (NLT).

Segun Adepoju

Note

Part Four

The Abundant Life

============

John 1:4 says that in Him was life, and that life was the light of all mankind. John 10:10 says, "... I have come that they may have life, and have it to the full." (NIV). The guarantee of the fullness of life is in God's abiding presence throughout your journey in life. In abundant life, you have total victory, royal dominion, assurance of answered prayers and long life.

===========================

10

The Total Victory

Thou shalt tread upon the lion and adder:
the young lion and the dragon shalt thou trample under feet. Psalm 91:13

There is no limit to our lives if we go through life with tenacity weeds, with strength of wildfire, and with the speed of God's direction. – Segun Adepoju, in *Getting Unstuck*

You cannot expect Victory and plan for defeat – Joel Osteen

I pursued my enemies and overtook them; And I did not turn back until they were consumed… Foreigners lose heart, And come trembling out of their strongholds.
Ps 18:37 &45, AMP

Psalm 91:13 is by no means presumptuous!

You are the master of whatever comes under your feet.

> Historically, after killing wild animals, most hunters would showcase their prowess and valiancy by stretching the dead animal on the ground. Sometimes they did this to measure the animal's length and other dimensions, especially to determine whether a record has been broken if killing such animals wasn't common.
>
> Some hunters have been seen posing with dead wild either by stepping on them or by climbing on them, especially if it's a lion. This is the posture of bravery and victory.

THE METAPHORS OF "LION," "SNAKE," AND "DRAGON"

Ordinarily, whatever you step on, should be subject to you. You can do whatever you like to it. Yet, no one would ordinarily step on a live lion or on a live serpent and not be in danger. This verse is by no means presumptuous or telling you to look for dangers of death by physically assaulting lions and dragons without commensurate weapons. You do not interpret spiritual words with ordinary senses.

Scripturally, roaring lions, snakes, dragons, etc. have been identified with the devil. In Genesis 3, the devil took the nature of a snake to deceive Eve. In 1 Peter 5:8, the devil is likened to a roaring lion, seeking whom he may devour. In chapter 12 of the Book of Revelation, dragon is likened to the devil.

In fact, the dragon and his evil angels lost to Archangel Michael in a fight. Revelation 12:9 says, "And the

> When God strikes the devil for your sake, victory looks cheap and unreal.

great dragon was cast out, that old serpent, called the Devil, and Satan, which deceiveth the whole world: he was cast out into the earth, and his angels were cast out with him."

I have cited above examples as guides to let you know that Satan is already a defeated foe. You should resist him based on this perspective.

The thrust of the metaphor in Psalm 91:3 is that "lion," "snake" and "dragon" symbolize the devil. When you are in God's family and abide by His terms and conditions, Satan should be under your feet (flatly defeated), especially when you exercise your faith in God to enforce your right of sonship and the victory attached to it.

It is reassuring to know that God's power is so great that His enemies bow down in fear before Him. (See Psalm 66:3, GNT).

David said that his enemies submitted to him. When God delivered him from the sword of his enemies, he sang of the Lord's deliverance, saying, "As soon as they hear of me, they shall obey me: the strangers shall submit themselves unto me. The strangers shall fade away, and be afraid out of their close places." (Psalm 18:44-45).

THE LORD IS THE SHOOTER, THE SAINTS CAN POSE

You can't match the devil with your natural skills and powers. It is God who fights spiritual warfare for you. The Psalmist prayed in Psalm 71:2-4, "Rescue me and deliver me...turn your ear to me and save me." Then he went on, "give the command to save me...Deliver me ... from the hand of the wicked, from the grasp of evil and cruel men." (NIV).

In Psalm 22:21, David prayed, "Rescue me from the mouth of the lions; save me from the horns of the wild oxen." (NIV).

David described God as the "LORD of hosts, the God of the armies of Israel." (I Sam 17:45). In other words, God is the Grand Commander of the Armies (Angels) of heaven. Moses also testified,

"The LORD is a warrior; The LORD is His name." (Exd 15:3, AMP). Even Satan recognized this and told Jesus, "... for it is written, He shall give his angels charge concerning thee." (Matt 4:6). God is the best fighter; he's the omniscient, the omnipotent, and the omnipresent!

It is after God has defeated the lion, snake, and dragon before you (collectively, the devils) that you can mess with and step on them. David describes the way God strikes the enemies this way: "But God shall shoot at them with an arrow; suddenly shall they be wounded. So they shall make their own tongue to fall upon themselves..." (Psalm 64:7-8).

Have you noticed that a clear sign of a dead wild animal is that its tongue shoots out like that of a thirsty dog?

When God strikes the devil for your sake, victory looks cheap and unreal; you live an unbelievable life just as stepping on lion and adder sounds weird to the ordinary ears. This is the peak of victory.

You have overcome anything that is under your feet! I John 5:4 says, "because everyone who has been born from God has won the victory over the world. Our faith is what wins the victory over the world." (GW). The "world" symbolizes a system (of the world) that disobeys God's words and instructions. Babylon scripturally represents the system of the world that is an affront to God's order. Compare Genesis 1:28 with Genesis 11:4.

During the millennial reign when Jesus would reign over the earth for a thousand years, the Satan would be prohibited from sharing the earth with Christ. Satan would be chained and banished to the bottomless pit for that period. The Bible calls the Satan, "dragon" that old serpent [of primeval times], who is the devil." Revelation 20:2, AMP. Satan is a defeated foe!

MORE THAN CONQUEROR

Romans 8:37 assures that in all these things we are more than conquerors through Christ who loved us and died for us.

> The Greek word, *hupernikao* means "more than conqueror." These are from the words, hyper which means "beyond" and nikko which means "conquer", respectively. Taken together, hupernikao connotes overwhelming victory; it's beyond a mere victory.

Why would Paul say that your victory is "beyond" in Romans 8:37? The victory that Christ won for you by His death is surpassing, exceeding, and it's the greatest ever.

Your victory is greater than victory over troubles of life itemized in Romans 8:35 (tribulation, distress, persecution, famine, nakedness, peril, or sword). One may have victory over an illness today and a few weeks or years later, get knocked down by the same illness.

One may have victory over the afflictions of life and yet get overrun with sin and its power. Such a victory can't be said to be overwhelming.

> During FIFA World Cup 2022 in Qatar, we saw some teams that started or ended the first half winning but came behind at the final whistle and eventually lost the game. Their "victory" wasn't *hupernikao*. Even the team that eventually won the trophy couldn't be said to have *hupernikao* because there's no guarantee that they'll qualify for the next World Cup let alone win the trophy yet again.
>
> When you are more than a conqueror however, you have victory over sins (and eternal death) even when afflictions seem to buffet you or take you away in death. You have victory over eternal death because you have victory over sin! Victory over sin through the finished work of Christ Jesus is *hupernikao*!

The sense of overwhelming victory might have persuaded Paul to declare in verses 38 and 39 that, "neither death, nor life, nor angels, nor principalities, nor powers, nor things present, nor things to come, nor height, nor depth, nor any other creature, shall be able to separate us from the love of God, which is in Christ Jesus our Lord."

Indeed, the victory in the *secret place* - under the shadow of God's glory - is overwhelming and calls for celebration!

UNDER YOUR FEET

In case you are still in doubt as to the connection between your status in God and Psalm 91:13, just hang on a second.

You are God's family member if you are a part of the church (the body of Christ), right? Ephesians 1:22-23 says, "And God placed all things under his feet and appointed him to be head over everything for the church, which is his body, the fullness of him who fills everything in every way." (NIV). If you're in Jesus Christ and everything is under Jesus' feet, then, Satan is under your feet - you are more than a conqueror!

Psalm 91:7 says that a thousand shall fall at your side, ten thousand at your right hand; but it shall not come near you. Verse 13 says that you will trample under your feet, lion and adder: the young lion and the dragon.

Here's the clincher. After God has incapacitated the dangers before you, they become nothing. With crown of victory on your head, the promise of living in God's right hand in heaven, and with your "right hand" status on earth, you can't but have Satan and his agents under your feet! Hallelujah!

SOMETHING TO THINK ABOUT

Reflection Point	Your total victory is determined by the extent you let God fight for you. You can never overemphasize the importance of divine guidance in fighting life afflictions!
Scripture Focus	Proverbs 3:5 - Trust in *and* rely confidently on the LORD with all your heart and do not rely on your own insight *or* understanding. (AMP)

Note

_____
_____
_____
_____
_____
_____
_____
_____
_____

11

The Right of Hand of God

Do not fear [anything], for I am with you;
Do not be afraid, for I am your God.
I will strengthen you, be assured I will help you;
I will certainly take hold of you with My righteous right hand [a hand of justice, of power, of victory, of salvation].'
Is 41:10, AMP.

God, your name is known everywhere; all over the earth people praise you. Your right hand is full of goodness. Ps. 48:10, NCV

who has gone into heaven and is at the right hand of God [that is, the place of honor and authority], with [all] angels and authorities and powers made subservient to Him. 1 Pet 3:22, AMP

God exalted Him to His right hand as Prince and Savior *and* Deliverer, in order to grant repentance to Israel, and [to grant] forgiveness of sins.
Acts 5:31, AMP

In God's household, membership comes with certain status symbol which is like a trademark reserved for distinction. The symbol is also like a code which is described with many words or expressions. One of such is the use of God's right hand.

Dwelling in God's Secret Place

As a young believer, I used to imagine God sitting on a big, beautiful, and glorious throne (and I still do) with Jesus Christ sitting resplendently in His right hand. Since Jesus had gone to heaven to prepare a place so we could be where He is (at the right hand of God), I would imagine myself sitting in God's right hand.

> The questions then follow: is God's throne in the center of heaven? If yes, and if Jesus and redeemed family members are in God's right hand, then, who or what would be in the left, back, and front of the throne?

Then Scriptures like Matthew 25:33 and Revelation 4:4 would throw a big stone and cause splash in the river of my mind. Hughh!

In Matthew 25:33, Jesus said that He would put the sheep (the righteous) on His right and the goats (the unrighteous) on His left. After the "hearing," He would then condemn the unrighteous to eternal damnation and the righteous would have eternal life. Does this then mean that the left side would be "empty" after the judgment?

Then, Revelation 4:4 tells us that twenty-four elders' thrones *surround* God's throne. This means that right and left, front and back sides of God's thrones will be occupied by the saints (family members), not just the right hand of God.

So then, where do we find a balance?

Over the years, some Scriptures modified (or expanded) my imagination. Whenever I come across Scriptures about God's right hand (or His righteous right hand), I see other things used together with it, which could probably amplify its possible interpretation.

Mark 16:19 and I Peter 3:22 tell us that Jesus Christ had gone into heaven and is at the right hand of God. The Bible also says that God's throne is in heaven. Hebrews 1:3 says that after "achieving forgiveness for the sins of all human beings, Jesus sat down in heaven at the right side of God, the Supreme Power." (GNT). God's Word version says Jesus "...now holds the honored position..." (GW).

Jesus fought and won to win the honor. So also must all believers, before they can sit at the right side of God in heaven. Psalm 16:11 says that God's presence is full of joy and that there's eternal pleasures at His right hand.

WHAT IS THE RIGHT HAND OF GOD?

David was moved by the Holy Spirit and wrote Psalm 110. In this classic Psalm we read how

God told His Son, Christ Jesus, to sit at God's right hand until He (God) subjugates His enemies. He would rule with His scepter (symbol of royal, sovereign power).

Jesus' *father* would trace His lineage to David, the King in Zion. His reign would be eternal (endless). In verse 5, we understand that, because Jesus is in God's right hand, He would crush kings (defeat the leaders of the system of the world), and this He would do triumphantly. This will literally happen during the millennial reign. However, the use of God's right hand here is in connection with reigning, power, justice, freedom, and victory.

Before we get to heaven, I believe we have this status symbol of God's right hand in our pilgrimage throughout life on earth. Jesus says that in the world we'd have tribulation, but we should be of good cheer because He has overcome the world for us. (John 16:33). This is the status symbol of victory that we have, an expression which is part of the possible interpretation for God's right hand.

When we work through life and its hurdles, we know that we're on the side of victory because, by our faith, we have overcome the world, and that we're in *the right hand of God, from the present life to life hereafter where we will reign with Jesus Christ evermore.*

According to Paul, when he visited Jerusalem to meet with James, Peter, and John (pillars of Jerusalem church), he was given "the right hand of fellowship." (Galatians 2:9). According to Jews' culture, this meant a recognition of someone with trust, confidence, and honor.

> In the Bible, the use of God's right hand (or God's righteous right hand) is not only in connection with the place of the righteous in heaven but is also associated with justice, righteousness, protection, victory, reigning, royalty, delight, honor, power, pardon, and salvation.
>
> For further study, see Hebrews 1:3 & 13; Isaiah 41:10; Psalm 118:15 & 16; Psalm 98:1; Psalm 44:3.

ONLY GOD CAN GRANT ACCESS TO HIS RIGHT HAND

Accessing God's right hand is not by being born into "Christian" family nor being *christened* on the eighth day of your birth. It's not attained by church or "Christian" program attendance, huge

Dwelling in God's Secret Place

financial donations to charity, and bearing "Christian" names.

Since His right hand is *in* the *secret place,* it's only God who can give it when you meet *"the righteousness requirement in Christ Jesus.* See Romans chapter 8.

In Mark 10, Zebedee's sons, James and John, asked Jesus to grant them the right to sit - one on Jesus' right hand, and the other on His left hand, in His glory. (Verse 37). But Jesus' answer is quite illuminating. "But to sit on my right hand and on my left hand is not mine to give; but it shall be given to them for whom it is prepared." (Verse 40).

> Accessing God's right hand is not by being born into "Christian" family nor by being christened on the eighth day of your birth.

Jesus attained the "right hand status" not by sudden flight to stardom, nor by being born to Jews' family but by obedience to His father, endurance of shame associated with His purpose, vicarious death, and by His resurrection.

In the parable of the sheep and goats, Jesus said that when He comes in His heavenly glory, He would separate the sheep from goats – sheep in the right and goats in the left. The king would tell those on the right, "Come, ye blessed of my Father, inherit the kingdom prepared for you from the foundation of the world." (Matt 25:34). Those on the right side chose salvation and produced the fruit of the Spirit. (Read further Matthew 25:31-46).

BEING AT JESUS' "PLACE"

Jesus wants us to be in the "place" where He is. If it is interpreted to be in heaven, then, that's fine because ultimately all believers would want to reign honorably and gloriously with Him eternally. After resurrection appearances, Jesus went to heaven and sat at the right hand of the father. (Mk 16:19). And if the "place" refers to *the right of sonship* conferred on us at salvation, then, that's also fine because without this *right*, we'll never access His house, whether in heaven or on earth.

Whichever way, the *place* has connection with the "right hand of God" or *"Jesus' status"* and it's very powerful, glorious, and honorable. Jesus' *status* after resurrection has been of victory over sin and over eternal death; being above the elemental wickedness of the universe; the permanent, honorable right of sonship. This begins with your status and becomes a *positional right* from the moment of your salvation through to heaven where you continue to reign with God eternally.

> "The right hand of God" begins with your status and *positional right* from the moment of your salvation through to heaven where you continue to reign with God eternally.

The terms and conditions of the place prepared for you are "new," "living," and "sacred." If you rented a property, you'd sign lease terms which you are required to observe. Otherwise, you are liable to be evicted. Dwelling in the *secret place* has similar principles, and the first step is salvation. That is the *secret place* of the Most High (God) referenced in Ps 91:1.

The death and resurrection of Jesus Christ opened this new and living way for us. (See Hebrews 10:20).

In this (secret) *place* you have all sorts of benefits and privileges (divine blessings), including divine protection from all disasters and evils of this world. There you also have your positional status – that is, who you are by reason of Jesus' perfected work of salvation. You become holy; an heir and a beneficiary of His inheritance; you are elevated higher beyond the elemental spirits of the universe. (See Ephesians 1:1-23 and Colossians 2:9-15).

It will interest you to know further that this "right hand" status in God which Jesus has prepared for you, comes with power and victory over the devil and his agents.

Ephesians 1:20-21 says that God "... raised Christ from the dead and seated him in the place of honor at God's right hand in heaven, far, far above any other king or ruler or dictator or leader. God's honor is far more glorious than that of anyone else either in this world or in the world to come." (TLB). The King James Version says, God set Jesus at God's "own right hand in the heavenly places, far above all principality, and power, and might, and dominion, and every name that is named, not only in this world, but also in that which is to come."

The "right hand" position speaks of the place or status of honor, repute, and dignity. It's what you can modernly call "honor roll." Aren't you glad it's been prepared once and for all?

SOMETHING TO THINK ABOUT

| **Reflection Point** | Jesus lived to conquer eternal death and live in glory. This is an eternal victory that was sealed with His blood for as many who would *receive* Him. |

Dwelling in God's Secret Place

	As God's family member here on earth, your status symbol is God's right hand – that of victory, honor, power, and pardon.
Scripture Focus	Ps 48:10: God, your name is known everywhere; all over the earth people praise you. Your right hand is full of goodness. NCV

Note

12

The Royal Dominion

> Because he hath set his love upon me, therefore will I deliver him: I will set him on high, because he hath known my name. Ps 91:14

A royal status is known for power, influence, and wealth.

There used to be a maxim in England in the fifteenth century that the King could do no wrong (because he was under no man). Even though the influence of the maxim has whittled down (because the King is under God and of course, the law made him the king), the royal domain in England is full of influence and privileges. For example, more than 4.1 billion broadcast audience reportedly watched the burial of the late Quen Elizabeth II[9]. During her lifetime, she visited about 110 countries across six continents. She was a global influence, diplomatically, and culturally.

This chapter talks about your intrinsic royal status in God's family and the blessings that come with it. Psalm 91:4 says that God will set you on high. It takes a higher person to set another person high. The "high" status isn't about living in higher topography or far above in the sky. We're talking about your spiritual class.

CONDITIONS TO ROYAL TREATMENT

Here we have two conditions namely, setting your love on God and knowing His name. Let's discuss them briefly.

Setting Your Love Upon God

In chapter 3, we talked briefly on this as condition to abiding in God's house.

> Love is the strongest, most powerful force in life. It's probably the sweetest word ever - either in human history or in any language.
>
> A lot of emotions are attached to love. Even though, ironically, humanity has used it to bring untold pains, it has brought many joys and fulfillment because its force can break barriers. God Himself is love!

Love lends itself to so many interpretations and meanings. Between romantic lovers, it may be misinterpreted as lust, sensuality, infatuation, or fun.

Between parents and children, it might be misunderstood to mean indulgence or obsession. Between politicians/public administrators, and the public, it might mean no more than mere sweet words to gain certain advantages. The list goes on! Even though it's often used to mean affection, tender care, or charity, the bottom line is that genuine love comes from the heart and is often associated with giving something of value rather than receiving.

God so *loved* the world and *gave* Jesus, His only Son, to save anyone who believes in Him. (John 3:16). We also ought to love Him and give Him our lives. (See I John 3:11-20, especially verse 16).

When you set your love on God, you would give Him preference in all that you do, including your decisions and how you spend your time. You would honor Him, His name, and His words. You would not hurt Him. You would speak well of Him to others. You would obey Him and that's the point you begin to enjoy His blessings in Psalm 91 and in other portions of the Scriptures.

According to Jesus, "… If anyone [really] loves Me, he will keep My word (teaching); and My Father will love him, and We will come to him and make Our dwelling place with him." (John 14:23, AMP).

Imagine the level of protection and security when God and Jesus (with all their angels) make their dwelling with you (through the Holy Spirit)! Don't think of this as having additional two or three unseen guests hanging around your lobby. You have the entire world and heavens!

The more you love God, the more you do for Him and care for others. In fact, what you do for others is evidence of your knowledge of and love for Him. The Bible tells us that "Love worketh no ill to his neighbour: therefore love is the fulfilling of the law." (Romans 13:10).

When you reciprocate God's gesture of love by setting your love on Him – by making Jesus, His son, your Savior – He would deliver you from any form of oppression, including sins, bad addictions, bad and failing health, failures, and premature death.

Happily, everything about Jesus is a means to deliver you – His blood, name, word, love, etc. I Peter 1:18-19 tells us that we were redeemed by the precious blood of Christ. Acts 4:12 tells us that "Salvation is found in no one else, for there

> To be sure, God's promise of deliverance in Psalm 91:14 is more than mere protection from physical dangers. It also covers deliverance from sin, the greatest of all dangers.
>
> As in the case of fear, sin does not come alone but with all manners of evils – sicknesses, diseases, death, etc. It's an amazing reality that our love for God can give us power, joy, and victory.

is no other name under heaven given to mankind by which we must be saved." (NIV). Philippians 2:10 says that at the name of Jesus every knee must bow. In John 6:63, Jesus says His words are full of the Spirit and life. And John 8:32 assures that we shall know the truth and the truth (His word) will set us free.

Your love for God provokes royal treats and blessings.

Knowing God's Name

A name is a means of identity. It speaks of ancestry, family, reputation, and values.

Philippians 2:9-11 teaches that every tongue must confess and openly acknowledge that Jesus Christ is the Lord. In *Getting Unstuck,* under the law of identity, I stated that what you identify yourself with, either exposes you to danger or protects you. I stated further that your *"identity is either an assess or a liability. Your name is your identity."*[10] God's name should be your constant identity.

There are many manifestations or revelations of God's name throughout the Bible such as: Yahweh:

- Nissi (The Lord, our Banner) - Exodus 17:5
- Jireh (The Lord will provide) - Genesis 22:14
- Shammah (The Lord is there) - Ezekiel 48:35
- Tsidqenu (The Lord our Righteousness) - Jeremiah 23:6
- Rapha (The Lord who heals) - Exodus 15:26
- El-Shaddai or Eloim (The Lord Almighty) - Genesis 1:1
- Elyon (The Lord, the Most High God) - Genesis 14:22
- El-Sabaoth (The Lord of Host, a military term used for the Commander of soldiers). This is

the name that David used to fight and overcome Goliath. I Samuel 17:45.

The list goes on!

God's names are not exhaustive. God is not done with manifesting Himself in different ways. All you need is to develop a deeper relationship with Him, and He would surely reveal and manifest diverse dimensions of His names (characters) to you. "Knowing" here isn't academic memorization of His name but a personal, deeper knowledge that's borne out of relationship and worship.

When you know God's name you would *acknowledge* Him and identify with Him – in your good and bad times. And that would trigger the following reactions from within you:

- Calling on His name for salvation – asking Him to save you (like a blind beggar in Luke 18:35-43)
- Calling His name for protection from dangers, as David did in I Samuel 17:45.
- Honoring His word and not profane or use it deceitfully.
- Trusting in the efficacies of the death and resurrection of His son, Jesus Christ.
- Continued obedience to His instructions.

As you trust in God and set your love on Him, He equips you with extraordinary strength so that you can fly and live beyond the reach of your spiritual predators. As you identify with Jesus Christ and His ancestry (God) in holiness and obedience to His words, He takes you as a priority in His protection. Proverbs 18:10 says that the name of the LORD is a strong tower: the righteous runs into it, and is safe."

ROYAL TREATS

Setting you on high

God is the King of kings. Jesus is the Prince of peace (Isaiah 9:6), even though He has been revealed as a Prophet and will yet be revealed as the King of kings and Lord of Lords (Revelation 17:14). Members of God's family are Jesus' brothers and sisters (Hebrew 2:11; Mark 3:34). And since we are joint heirs with Christ, we're princes of God who is the King of heaven.

> Members of God's family are Jesus' brothers and sisters (Hebrew 2:11; Mark 3:34).

Galatians 4:6-7 says, "And because ye are sons, God hath sent forth the Spirit of his Son into your hearts, crying, Abba, Father. Wherefore thou art no more a servant, but a son; and if a son, then an heir of God through Christ."

In Luke 10, Jesus had sent out seventy evangelists two-by-two on a mission. Upon their return, the evangelists reported to Jesus that the demons submitted to them in Jesus' name. In response, Jesus said that He "saw Satan falling from heaven as a flash of lightning!" (Luke 10:18, TLB). The evangelists worked in obedience. God lifted them high and put Satan under them.

The blessing of being sent on high is not only about promotion at work or in business; it's more about your potential place of operation above the devil and his demons.

Ephesians 6:12 tells us that we don't wrestle against flesh and blood, but against principalities, against powers, against the rulers of the darkness of this world, against spiritual wickedness in high places. Salvation in Christ Jesus elevates your status higher above evil spirits. You are thus born into a kingdom of absolute dominion.

The high place being assured here is a place of victory and rest where your strength is renewed. Isaiah 40:31 tells us that they that wait upon the Lord (depend on God, obey God, pray to God for guidance and directions) shall renew their strength. They shall mount up with wings like eagles; they shall run and not be weary; they shall walk and not faint.

Why would God compare you to an eagle?

First remember that God created you and is the one who created eagle as well. An eagle is the only bird that can look in the direction of the sun and keep flying while its pursuers fall away. It is focused and this makes it hit its target prey successfully.

In Exodus 19:4, God instructed Moses to tell the Israelites how he (God) carried the Israelites on "eagles' wings" and brought them to himself. What about eagles' wings? In the storm, no animal can fly like an eagle. Its special wings are very strong in balancing its movements in the space. This giant bird is a symbol of unusual strength, and its wings are a metaphor for divine protection.

Royal Deliverance

The word "deliver" in Hebrew is *Yasah*, a verb which means to *ransom, redeem, rescue or salvage*. They all describe a situation where one is freed from an oppressor and released to another hand (of peace and freedom).

God is *Yahweh* (great redeemer) and that's why His Son, Jesus Christ is the redeemer.

While there are many ways in which God delivered His people from their enemies before Jesus manifested, the only constant means has been His Word. He would command the prophets, priests, and kings (as intermediaries) and these officials would carry it out and Israelite would be saved. (See Hebrews 1:1). This Word manifested in the flesh and is called Jesus. (See Matthew 1:21; John 1.1-2, 14).

Whether in the Old or New Testament, the word of God has been the major means by which God delivers His people from the hands of their enemies.

The devil is the number one enemy – the oppressor - even though he uses human beings and his demons as subterfuge. Ultimately, God sent Jesus to put an end to devil's works. I John 3:8 says that "... the Son of God was manifested, that he might destroy the works of the devil." Isn't that what God promised in Psalm 91:14?

Once sin is dealt with, the associated dangers are extinguished. David was pleading that God should not rebuke him in His anger because at that moment, he was in pains. Then he said, "There is no soundness in my flesh because of Your indignation; There is no health in my bones because of my sin." (Ps 38:3, AMP).

1 Chronicles 10:13 tells us that King "Saul died for his transgression which he committed against the Lord, even against the word of the Lord, which he kept not, and also for asking counsel of one that had a familiar spirit, to enquire of it." Here sin brought death.

Similarly, 1 Chronicles 9:1 says that the people of Judah were taken captive to Babylon because of their unfaithfulness. (NIV). Here, sin brough captivity.

May you not be victims of devil's destructions.

Thanks to God's salvation that has opened a great door of deliverance and victory for us!

SOMETHING TO THINK ABOUT

| **Reflection Point** | It's not enough to be borne into a royal family. You must abide by the rules of the kingdom. Even Jesus Christ, though having the nature of God, still obeyed the Kingdom rules before being set on high by God. |

| Scripture Focus | **Philippians 2:5-11** – "In your relationships with one another, have the same mindset as Christ Jesus ... Therefore God exalted him to the highest place and gave him the name that is above every name..." (NIV). |

Note

13

Blessed Assurance -

The Right of Answered Prayers

> He shall call upon me, and I will answer him: I will be with him in trouble;
> I will deliver him, and honor him. Psalm 91:15

> Because I called and you refused [to answer],
> I stretched out my hand and no one has paid attention
> [to my offer]; Then they will call upon me (Wisdom), but I will not answer;
> They will seek me eagerly but they will not find me. Prov 1:24 & 28, AMP

In literature, repetition plays the role of emphasis. The same goes for biblical hermeneutics.

When you see many words repeated in a context, it means there's a point being emphasized which must be noted and understood. In Psalm 91:15 alone, God repeated "I will" three times and these are in response to a call on Him. Among other things, God wants to reassure you that He has irrevocably committed Himself to answering you when you call upon Him from a pure heart.

CALLING UPON GOD

In chapter 3, we learned that it's not everyone who calls on God that gets answers but those who call in the name of Jesus Christ. In other words, we must obey God if we want Him to answer our calls.

> In literature, repetition plays the role of emphasis.

The Book of Proverbs contains words of wisdom (divine wisdom to guide humanity) and not a collection of earthly wisdom. The Bible tells us that Jesus Christ is the power of God and the wisdom of God.

Proverbs 1 is a call of Wisdom. It says, "Because I called and you refused [to answer], I stretched out my hand and no one has paid attention [to my offer]; And you treated all my counsel as nothing. And would not accept my reprimand, I also will laugh at your disaster; I will mock when your dread *and* panic come..."

The Wisdom continued, "Then they will call upon me (Wisdom), but I will not answer; They will seek me eagerly but they will not find me, Because they hated knowledge And did not choose the fear of the LORD [that is, obeying Him

Dwelling in God's Secret Place

with reverence and awe-filled respect] ..." Then He concluded, "But whoever listens to me (Wisdom) will live securely *and* in confident trust and will be at ease, without fear *or* dread of evil." (See Proverbs 1:24-33, AMP).

God can protect you from all evils of life without you having to pray to Him. But He knows that you need more than "things" to fulfil your purpose in life. Primarily, you need Him. And one certain way you can find Him and know His mind and way, is by a cooperative relationship.

> You would notice that Psalm 91:15 doesn't say "he shall pray to me..." but "he shall call upon me." The former speaks of making a request in form of conversation (praying to Him might be part of worship) while the latter connotes worship – a shared experience where you give yourself and things of value to God, pleasing Him, referencing, adoring, and ascribing greatness to Him.
>
> When God is pleased with you, He'll be pleased with your offering. He'll also make His *mind* and *ways* known to you by His Spirit and His word.

In Bible interpretation, when a word is first used or mentioned in the Bible, you interpret it within the context of usage. Calling upon the Lord and calling upon the name of the Lord mean the same thing. To "call upon the Lord" (usually in KJV) was first used in the Bible, in Genesis 4:26, then in chapters 12:8, 13:4; 21:33 and then in 26:25.

In Genesis 4:26 God had granted Adam another son (Seth) in place of Abel who was killed by Cain. Seth gave birth to Enosh. And at that time, men began "to call upon the name of the LORD."

In Genesis 12:8, after God had called him, Abram travelled to Canaan and settled in Moreh at Shechem where the Lord appeared to him and promised that his descendants would inherit the land (Canaan). There, Abram "...built an altar to the LORD and called on the name of the LORD." (NIV).

In Genesis 26, Isaac had become very wealthy, and this led to jealousy from Abimelech King of Gerar who sent him away. He dug two wells (Esek and Sitnah) but again he moved to another place due to opposition. After the third well (Rehoboth), he began to flourish and went to Bersheba where God reassured him of His abiding presence. In Genesis 26:25, Isaac built an "altar there, and called upon the name of the LORD.

In each of the above scriptural references, one thing is common and that is worship of God. Some other translations actually used the word "worship." For example, Genesis 4:26 says, "... At that time people began to worship the Lord." (GW). According to Good News Translations, "... It was then that people began using the Lord's holy name in worship."

Worship isn't a haphazard chore; our souls and spirits are involved in their transformed states. That's why Romans 12:2 says that we should not conform to the superficialities of the world but to be "transformed *and* progressively changed [as you mature spiritually] by the renewing of your mind [focusing on godly values and ethical attitudes]" so that we may prove for ourselves "what the will of God is, that which is good and acceptable and perfect [in His plan and purpose" for us. (AMP). This is when our worship is *live* and not dead!

> Worship is more than singing slow or fast songs. It's even more than offering sacrifices.

> Authentic scriptural worship of the almighty God begins with surrendering of your total will and being to Him - spirit, soul, and body. Romans 12:1 says that we should present our "bodies [dedicating all of yourselves, set apart] as a living sacrifice, holy and well-pleasing to God, which is your rational (logical, intelligent) act of worship." (AMP).
>
> We can't worship God in our adamic nature but in a transformed state that conforms to the status of Christ that we're meant to be in God's family.

When you first seek relationship with God, every other blessing follows. 2 Corinthians 6:14-17 urges us to come out of the worldliness (sinful system of the world). God's Spirit that we carry doesn't have any fellowship with evil spirits in the world. The Bible commands us, "... come out from among them, and be ye separate, saith the Lord, and touch not the unclean thing; and I will receive you. And will be a Father unto you, and ye shall be my sons and daughters, saith the Lord

Almighty." (II Cor 6:17-18). It's this parent-child relationship that God wants to keep with you.

Any stranger may request a favor from (or praying to) your dad, but it takes the child to relate with him, go to his closet, or inhabit his house. God wants more than a prayer relationship from you; He wants a parent-child relationship where you can lay your heart bare before Him and not be ashamed.

I WILL ANSWER HIM: I WILL BE WITH HIM IN TROUBLE; I WILL DELIVER HIM, AND HONOUR HIM

After you have established a genuine relationship in worship and service, God would answer your prayers in a way and at a time that make you fulfil your purpose in life (and not to consume it on your lust or for oppressing others). That's why God's answer matters the most. Whichever way it comes, you're assured of His presence.

There are three major things in life that define every human being. These are (a) *acceptability*, (b) *victory*, and (c) *honor*. All these are tied to the word "answer" as you'd see below.

Acceptability

Conflicts begin when your expectations and experiences don't match.

Actions, reactions, questions, or requests are the mother of expectations. Whoever you are – President, King, Bishop, chief executive officer, servants, employees, husband, wife, son, daughter – when you don't get what you want, or when you get snubbed, you become livid with anger, get unsettled, and in some cases, become despondent. You feel unacceptable; you feel less than others. In this condition, many have committed suicide or committed crimes. But when you have answers to your requests, you feel energized, hopeful, and ready to act.

Every human being needs acceptability that comes from *answers*.

God knows that you need answers and that's why He makes this a first line of experience when you come into a *worship relationship* with Him. God's answer comes in different ways – Yes, No, or Wait. He may even tell you what he told apostle Paul, "... My grace is sufficient for thee: for my strength is made perfect in weakness." (II Cor 12:9).

> Those who seek God's face don't miss what's in His hands!

As God's verdict on David for his adultery with Bathsheba and murder of Uriah, God struck with illness, the child that Bathsheba had for David, and he later died.

For seven days, David fasted and prayed to God. His servants didn't know how to break the sad news to him. He had hoped that God would heal the boy. But when he suspected strange discussions among his servants, conflicts set in. He asked, "Is the child dead?" (2 Kings 12:15-19). And the answer was in the affirmative! What did he do next? Verse 20 says. "Then David got up from the ground. After he had washed, put on lotions, and changed his clothes, he went into the house of the LORD and worshiped. Then he went to his own house, and at his request they served him food, and he ate." (NIV).

David desperately wanted an answer to his prayers. He wanted to know what to do next. At that point, it didn't matter that he got a "NO" and as far as he was concerned a "NO" was an answer.

Whatever the nature or form of the answer, it's certainly better than waiting indefinitely!

Sometimes, it's not the specifics of the answer but the fact that we have the answer that calms our nerves - even if the answer isn't what we want!

Victory

The two greatest forces in life are pleasure and pain.

People generally prefer pleasure to pain (troubles). Jesus stated that in the world we would have troubles but that we should be of good cheer because He had overcome the world for us. God says He would be with you in troubles; He doesn't say you would not have troubles. Job 14:1 tells us that man that is born of a woman is of few days and full of trouble.

There's a difference between *not having troubles* and *getting out of troubles with God's help*. The former is at best a utopian state while the latter is scripturally guaranteed. Life is ordinarily full of troubles. You may not like it but that's a fact.

We would never appreciate God and His power if we never had to face and deal with troubles. Failures help us to value success.

The taste of good life makes us to run away from death. Knowledge of pleasure makes us detest pain. Troubles make us know the joy of victory and triumph.

> God could have said, "I will not let troubles get to you..." but instead said that He would "be with you in troubles." God's presence with you in trouble times creates for you, experiences of wisdom, maturity, and the joy of His presence.

Man would ordinarily live independently of God in the world without troubles. When Lucifer made troubles in heaven God dealt with Him. When Jesus was on earth, He dealt with and overcame troubles. In fact, He came to deal with sin, the greatest troubles, by nailing it to the cross. Isaiah's prophecy described Him as a man acquainted with sorrows.

When God promised to be with you in troubles, he offered himself to be part of your life one hundred percent – in troubles and in victory. Victory experience is what every human being desires. That's why he wants to walk with you every step you take in this world. He wants to counsel you, direct you, teach and mentor you in a close range such that you are trained in the art of fighting to have victory over every trouble of life. This is an invaluable relationship that guides you in the earthly sojourn to eternal life hereafter. God knows that you are not a programmed robot but a reflection of Himself.

David valued God's relationship as a means of overcoming troubles in Psalm 16. Unlike those with relationship with lesser gods, David put his trust in the almighty God, made the Lord the portion of his inheritance, had a working relationship with God by setting God before him always. See Psalm 16:9-11.

I hope you can savor this type of relationship that guarantees victory experiences.

Honor

I am yet to find anyone who doesn't want honor.

Semantically, there are some words with special meanings attached to them. "Honor" is one of them. You must have done something that is honorable before you can be honored. Alternatively, you must have associated with an honorable person. Honor is preceded by noble deeds, knowledge, and value. And most importantly, you must have been an honorable person before you could be honored. *It's in your "being" that honor becomes more valuable.*

Why would God honor you? You have trusted in Him. You are His child and a member of His family. And most importantly, you have a genuine relationship with Him which is evident in your relationship with other people.

To be honored is to be exalted and dignified in a

> There's a difference between "not having troubles" and "getting out of troubles with God's help."

unique way. God is honorable. By honoring you, He brings you to an exalted, royal position of relationship where you enjoy certain privileges. When valuable things are scarce in town, people prioritize honorable individuals by making reservations for them.

Your salvation puts you in an honorable position, but your continued obedience and child-father relationship preserve your honor.

In Luke 15, the prodigal (but repentant) son had demanded his inheritance and squandered it riotously in a foreign land. Then he came to his senses and made his way back to his loving, patient, and forgiving father who wasted no time in celebrating his "lost but found" son. Permit me to summarize the son's elevation to the honorable status with an excerpt from my book, *Getting Unstuck*.

> Having found and welcomed the lost son, the first thing the father did was to

change the son's dress – undress the robe of shame, penury, afflictions, and waywardness. He then exchanged them for a garment of honor, ring of dignity and shoe of nobility. Then the Party began. This is a royal welcome and apogee of a state of getting unstuck.

You 'll notice that the father gave the repentant son ... a royal treat. This was deliberate. The father here implies God, your heavenly father, while the repentant son represents you in your change of mind for better. What follows is your royal status.[11]

May you be found honorable before God and before men in Jesus' name!

> When God promised to be with you in troubles, he offered himself to be part of your life one hundred percent – in troubles and in victory.

SOMETHING TO THINK ABOUT

| **Reflection Point** | Our worship begins with the state of our hearts – our beings. Abel worshipped God with the finest offerings. Not so with Cain. The state of our |

	hearts influences the offerings in our hands!
Scripture Focus	**Genesis 4:3-5** – After some time Cain brought some of his harvest and gave it as an offering to the LORD. Then Abel brought the first lamb born to one of his sheep, killed it, and gave the best parts of it as an offering. The LORD was pleased with Abel and his offering, but he rejected Cain and his offering..." GNT.

Note

14

Long Life and Salvation

With long life will I satisfy him, and shew him my salvation. Psalm 91:16

There will be no miscarriages or infertility in your land, and I will give you long, full lives. Exodus 23:26, NLT.

My son, never forget the things
I've taught you. If you
want a long and
satisfying life,
closely follow
my instructions.
Proverbs 3:1-2, TLB.

Congratulations!

You're unstoppable, you know?

We have two major things left to discuss - long life and salvation.

Let's start with long life. But before then, let's talk about Psalm 90.

Dwelling in God's Secret Place

I am not sure I have ever met someone who wished to die young. If there was anyone wishing to die young, then it must be for sad reasons.

> It is not the calendar years that matter but the life you put in them.

Though life has its bad times, it has many interesting things to wish for, or live for - even for a longer time.

The question then is: what is a long life?

PSALM 90

One of the often-read scriptures in birthday celebrations is found in Psalm 90 (also written by Moses). Let's look at it in perspective.

Psalm 90:9-10 reads:

> For all our days are passed away in thy wrath: we spend our years as a tale that is told. The days of our years are threescore years and ten; and if by reason of strength they be fourscore years, yet is their strength labour and sorrow; for it is soon cut off, and we fly away.

Verse 12 says, "So teach us to number our days, that we may apply our hearts unto wisdom."

Moses wrote Psalm 90 as a reminiscence of wilderness experiences.

> God works with time and season while man invented and works with clock. How then can a limited, finite man use clock, or numbers of moon appearances to define his life or dictate to the unlimited, infinite God, how his life should be measured?

In Numbers chapter 13, most of the spies from Canaan exploration reported that the Israelites would not be able to attack the inhabitants to possess the land. Only Caleb and Joshua brought positive reports. The negative reports motivated the people to grumble against Moses. They wished they had died in their bondage in Egypt. They wanted to go back to bondage. They did not believe that God could do what He promised.

Chapter 14 tells us that the Israelites rebelled against God who determined to punish that generation. God said that not all of them would enter the promise land but that they would die in the wilderness.

One of the ways to eliminate the rebellious generation was that they would all perish from a certain age bracket. Numbers 14:29 says, "Your carcasses shall fall in this wilderness; and all that were numbered of you, according to your whole number, from twenty years old and upward which have murmured against me." Verses 33-34 says:

> "And your children shall wander in the wilderness forty years, and bear your whoredoms, until your carcasses be wasted in the wilderness. After the number of the days in which ye searched the land, even forty days, each day for a year, shall ye bear your iniquities, even forty years, and ye shall know my breach of promise."

If you do a bit of arithmetic, then you will discover that those who were 20 years and below at the time of God's declaration would be spared from death. The period of destruction would be 40 years. In effect, the children who were 20 years then would now be 60 years (threescores). For the fortunate ones who were 30 years then, after the said 40 years of destruction, they would be 70 years (threescores and ten).

PSALM 90:9-10 ISN'T MEANT FOR ALL

Moses' words in Psalm 90:9-10 should not be taken, read, and applied out of context. Even as at the time of God's declaration, it didn't apply to other nations and peoples. Neither did it apply to all people globally upon entrance into Canaan and up till date.

> Based on Numbers 14:29-34 and Psalm 90:9-10, the generation to which limited life span applied were rebellious; they dared God in the wilderness.

In fact, the limited life span prescription in Psalm 90:9-10 is more of a curse than casual words. As a member of God's family who has been redeemed from the curse of sin and who "has been crucified with Christ," you are exempted from its venom. Even if such a curse applies to any person that you know, then it ceases to have any force upon his membership in God's family.

Galatians 3:13 tells us that "Christ purchased our freedom *and* redeemed us from the curse of the Law *and* its condemnation by becoming a curse for us—for it is written, "CURSED IS EVERYONE WHO HANGS [crucified] ON A TREE (cross)." (AMP).

LONG LIFE

God is the author and giver of life; He determines the number of days in life for each one as He pleases.

> Relative to His purposes for your life, in God's reckoning, "long life" is the life that you need to fulfil purpose – whether it's less than thirty, less than fifty, or even more than a hundred years.
>
> In God's calculation, the "long life" that He promised you is your full length of days, your full lifespan, or using the Living Bible's rendition of Psalm 91:16, what God has promised is to satisfy you "… with a full life."
>
> The promised "full life" or "long life" or "good old days" for each one is relative and determined by God.

You would notice that God never defined "long life" throughout the Bible. Neither did He promise "long years." His measurement of what is "long" is different than ours.

Job, the Old Testament character who was blessed with wits and, wealth, said, "Since his days are determined, the number of his months is with You [in Your control], And You have made his limits so he cannot pass [his allotted time]." (Job 14:5, AMP).

To us, because many people in the Old Testament lived up to hundreds of years, we assume they had "long" years, but the Bible would call it "good old age." To God however, one thousand years is like one day. (2 Peter 3:18).

David became king at 30 (II Samuel 5:4) and reigned for 40 years. According to the Bible, he died "in a good old age "[his seventy-first year], full of days (satisfied), riches and honor." (I Chronicles 29:27, AMP). Here, David's "good old age" was about 70 years. However, Moses (who wrote Psalm 90:9-10) "... was a hundred and twenty years old when he died: his eye was not dim, nor his natural force abated." (Deuteronomy 34:7).

"Premature" or "Untimely" Death

You may want to ask, *"if a man dies in his thirties - in the prime of his life - is it God's full life for him ...?"* Frankly, I would not know whether that's a full life (only God knows), and to be sure, I will not pray that for myself or for my loved ones, and certainly not for you! While some scriptures tie long life to certain obedience, the definition of long life remains known to God alone.

One thing is certain: we might not know whether a toddler, or a teenager or even an adult who dies "prematurely" has fulfilled purpose before death, that doesn't mean or conclude that they died without fulfilling purpose. *Ignorance of a thing or an event does not conclude its nonexistence!*

Jesus died in His early thirties but fulfilled His purpose. (John 19:30). Apostle Paul died in His sixties. He, however, fulfilled his assignment. (II Timothy 4:7-8).

In Exodus 23:26, God promised His people: "There will be no miscarriages or infertility in your land, and I will give you long, full lives." (NLT) This assurance removes all doubts on whether God wants us "prematurely" or "untimely" dead. He wants us to grow in strength and years and into full old age. Jesus grew in wisdom and stature, and in favor with God and man. (Luke 2:52). Samuel also grew up. (I Samuel 2:26; 3:19).

God alone determines the exact length of days or years. *We should cooperate with Him with our willingness and obedience so we can achieve fulfillment within our allotted time.*

I would be remiss if I fail to acknowledge the fact that the devil might bring about "untimely" deaths and thereby potentially "disrupt" God's purposes for individuals.

The sundry instrumentalities through which the

devil frustrates purposes include sins, greed, falling into temptations, disobedience to God's instructions (and by extension, crime against the constituted authority), and hopelessness leading to suicide, to mention a few.

> God did not promise 60 years or 70 years to us. He promised His family members a long life – long enough to fulfil our respective purposes. To Him, it's not the number of years that confers fulfilment of purpose to mankind. Jesus Christ spent about thirty-three and a half years on earth and fulfilled His purpose.
>
> If 60 or 70 years were God's standard, then why didn't Jesus live up to 60 years? And, why did we have several thousands (if not millions) of people who lived beyond 70, 80, 90 and even a hundred years?
>
> If we all can be sure that we have at least up to 60 or 70 years, then we'd do whatever we like in our early years and then suddenly become "the friend of God" in our late 50s. It doesn't work that way!

Proverbs 3:1-2 says, "My son, never forget the things I've taught you. If you want a long and satisfying life, closely follow my instructions." (TLB).

Thus, keeping God's commandments can potentially prolong your life.

GOD'S SALVATION

The second leg of Psalm 91:16 says that God will show you His salvation. If you're still unsettled as to why God didn't promise you "many years" to "enjoy" life, or maybe you're wondering how you can still be happy, joyous, and victorious while in this evil world, then the last word of Psalm 91 will answer your question.

Showing You His Salvation

God's promise to "show" you His salvation means that He would let you experience His salvation.

In general, salvation means being saved, rescued, delivered, and salvaged. While any of these explains a person's experience of being rescued from the sting of sins at redemption, it also means that God will save (protect) you further from any evil during your membership in His family on earth.

Both interpretations explain how God secures His promise of long life for you. He would save you from falling into temptations. He would also save you from making wrong choices that could waste your life.

> The full lifespan of tomatoes fruit is in its seed. That of corn is also in its seed. Your lifespan is in your purpose and that's worth celebrating.
>
> Whether you know how many years you'll live or not, God's assurance is chilling – you'll live your full years. May you live your full years to fulfil your purpose in Jesus' name. Amen.

Teaching His disciples on how to pray, Jesus said in Matthew 6:13, "And don't let us yield to temptation, but rescue us from the evil one." (NLT). He may rescue you in many ways, including first giving you a revelation, counsel (from the Holy Spirit or God's ministers like pastors, prophets, etc.), or through direct written words in the Bible. The most important thing for you to note is that God will not leave you stranded; He'll save you at the nick of time.

Psalm 46:1 says, "God is our refuge and strength, an ever-present help in trouble."

Are you wondering how you'll be able to enjoy "long life" during life vicissitudes? Remember that Psalm 91:15 assures that God would be with you in trouble. Now, here's another one. Psalm 46:11 concludes, "The Lord Almighty is with us; the God of Jacob is our fortress."

When the Lord Almighty (Yahweh Eloim) who made the heaven and the earth assures you of His presence with the seal of "God of Jacob" (because the covenant of His abiding presence sworn with Jacob still stands) then you can't but experience His salvation.

SOMETHING TO THINK ABOUT

Reflection Point	Your purpose isn't in your years. But your years are in your purpose! It's what you do with your days, weeks, months, and years that determines the fulfilment of your purpose. Years are combinations of numbers. Long life or full life, or good old age are God's gifts to mankind and are measured relative to fulfilling God's assignments.
Scripture Focus	**Psalm 91:16**– "With long life will I satisfy him, and shew him my salvation."

| | **Proverbs 3:16** - "Long life is in her right hand; In her left hand are riches and honor." (AMP). |

Note

Postscript

He who dwells in the secret place of the Most high shall abide under the shadow of the Almighty.

Psalm 91's thematic lesson focuses on *abiding* in God's house (the secret place). John 14 assures believers in Christ that Jesus Christ had gone to prepare (and now He has prepared) a *place* for us in God's house. Then John 15 emphasizes the need for believers to *abide* in Christ, even as a branch must abide in the vine to be productive. The sense of *abiding* in Psalm 91:1 and in John 15 are the same. It talks about the inherent blessings *in* our salvation, and which makes our *dwelling* worthwhile.

The central cord that holds God's house and His family tightly for productivity is *relationship* - relationship among the members of the family horizontally and between the members and God, vertically. We're never complete in this current divide in eternity and even hereafter without healthy relationship with God.

Our fruitfulness begins and ends with doing what pleases God, the Head of the House.

The relationship we keep with one another is born out of love from pure hearts which ignites the beams of light that show the Way to the wasting world. By this, the world knows that we're Jesus' disciples. This is when God's love *makes* us epistles that the world reads. We serve, fellowship, and witness not out of idleness or for some personal gains but because of love which flows from God.

The father-child relationship between us and God is also borne out of love. We love Him because He first loved us with an everlasting love. We obey Him not out of fear but because we love Him.

As a genuine family member in God's house who wants to flourish, you must value a godly relationship which is evidenced by your *service* and your *worship*. You can't do one without the other. The goal of your relationships horizontally or vertically should be pure worship from your heart. This is more than burning incense and offering material sacrifices. It's rather offering of your *self* or adamic nature and purging it of any dross that might hinder you from enjoying the blessings in God's house.

It's not until God sees Himself in you that your worship becomes efficacious of a truly Kingdom-minded family member who's bound by an eternal love relationship.

Dwelling in God's Secret Place

> The essence of your worship while on earth is to conform you to God's nature which ultimately glorifies God. This makes *dwelling* in His house meaningful. After all, it's the nature of a specie that determines its habitat!

Let's take cover in God's secret place.

In God We Trust. July 4 of every year is very important to us as a people in the United States of America. Many things happen in life that we call coincidences. But I want to believe that it was not a coincidence that I got the inspiration for this book on July 4, 2020, in the heat of Covid-19 pandemic. May the Spirit of freedom in Christ work the wonder of healings to the victims worldwide, and may God comfort their families. May God's cover continue to protect us from all evils. Amen.

No matter the fury of any pandemic, Covid-19, Ebola virus or any other evil, we are assured of the maximum protection because in this life and hereafter, we *dwell* in God's secret place!

Psalm 91 (NKJV)

He who dwells in the secret place of the Most High
Shall abide under the shadow of the Almighty.
2 I will say of the LORD, "*He is* my refuge and my fortress;
My God, in Him I will trust."
3 Surely He shall deliver you from the snare of the fowler
And from the perilous pestilence.
4 He shall cover you with His feathers,
And under His wings you shall take refuge;
His truth *shall be your* shield and buckler.
5 You shall not be afraid of the terror by night,
Nor of the arrow *that* flies by day,
6 *Nor* of the pestilence *that* walks in darkness,
Nor of the destruction *that* lays waste at noonday.
7 A thousand may fall at your side,
And ten thousand at your right hand;
But it shall not come near you.
8 Only with your eyes shall you look,
And see the reward of the wicked.
9 Because you have made the LORD, *who is* my refuge,
Even the Most High, your dwelling place,
10 No evil shall befall you,
Nor shall any plague come near your dwelling;
11 For He shall give His angels charge over you,
To keep you in all your ways.
12 In *their* hands they shall bear you up,
Lest you dash your foot against a stone.
13 You shall tread upon the lion and the cobra,
The young lion and the serpent you shall trample underfoot.
14 "Because he has set his love upon Me, therefore I will deliver him;
I will set him on high, because he has known My name.
15 He shall call upon Me, and I will answer him;
I *will be* with him in trouble;
I will deliver him and honor him.
16 With long life I will satisfy him,
And show him My salvation.

Other Books by the Author

GETTING UNSTUCK
WORKBOOK AND BIBLE STUDY

About the Book

Getting Unstuck Workbook and Bible Study is a great tool for practical godly character development and spiritual growth for individuals and organizations. Churches, Christian Ministries and Fellowships would find this Workbook exceedingly useful for teaching, edification, discussion and reference materials.

This Workbook is a useful learning material and guide for mentors and mentees as it contains self studies and reflection points for:

- Goal setting
- Problem solving
- Growth indices, and
- In-depth Bible study.

It is a perfect fit for both goal-specific and general purpose mentoring programs.

Itinerary ministers, Bible students in colleges and Theological schools, Pastors, and Bible Teachers would pleasantly find this Workbook as a useful companion.

Getting Unstuck Workbook and Bible Study exhaustively covers all the 13 critical principles of success discussed in Getting Unstuck, authored by Segun Adepoju.

About the Author

Segun Adepoju is a teacher of God's Word. His apostolic calling came with exceptional teaching and pastoral anointing. He likes to teach in churches, conferences, seminars, campuses, and fellowships.

Segun is passionately committed to discipleship and leadership in the body of Christ. He loves to discuss and teach principles on any area of human endeavors from the Bible.

He is a foreign trained attorney with a specialized master's degree (LL.M) in Tax Law from the University of Houston Law Center. He's also a member of the Association of International Petroleum Negotiators (AIPN). He's happily married to his long time friend and classmate, Christy, blessed with children and based in the United States.

SEGUN ADEPOJU

GETTING UNSTUCK
WORKBOOK AND BIBLE STUDY

Index

A

abide	14, 19, 27, 52, 132, 191
activate	16
administrator	152
Adullam	107
aerodynamic	55
Africa	51
Agag	46
Agriculture (tropical)	51
all things (under)	138
anatomical(ly)	43, 117
ancestry	155, 157
angels	13, 80, 118, 122, 123, 124, 138, 153
animals	29, 55, 79, 80, 111, 131
answered	33, 46, 57, 129, 163
Apostles	33, 67
appearances	40, 146, 180
Arrows/arrows	34, 61, 86, 92, 98, 134
Asaph	59

B

bait(s)	119, 120, 121, 128
banana (tree, leaves)	55
believers	32, 36, 111, 142, 146, 191
Boaz	57, 113
body of Christ	138
brothers (Jesus' brothers)	157
buckler	77, 86, 87

C

calling unto (God)	111
calling upon (God, the Lord)	164, 166,
calling His name	156
Canaan	166, 180, 182
catalyst	74

character	23, 46, 113, 156, 183,
chick(s)	77, 79, 80
child (of God)	16, 27, 123,
children	152, 169, 77, 81, 101, 117, 119, 122, 181
choice (s)	32, 104, 114, 188, 195
choose(s)	32, 42, 44, 108, 111, 114, 165
church	15, 25, 26, 36, 138, 144,
command(s)	40, 7 2, 118, 133, 160, 168,
commandment(s)	11, 27, 56, 62, 64, 187
communication	109

condition(s)
    to abiding 37
    to dwelling 30
    to royal treatment 151
    Notes on the Conditions 41
    Psalm 91 Conditions 38
corruption 23
covenant
    God's 58, 60
    Lord's 72
    Of His abiding presence 189
    relationship 25
    respect for 59
    speaks 57

cover
    for reptiles 29
    of God's glory 52
    protective 73, 86
covering
    by feather and wings 79
    from danger 39
    glorious 191
    God's 12, 57, 61, 72, 77
    Great 77
    His 52
    great 12, 191
    in the secret place 47
    our 71
    of a shelter 46

D

darkness	22, 71, 92, 98, 158,
David	15, 40, 53, 70, 83, 106-110, 161, 184
dazzle	65, 74
descendants	166
disciples	13, 20, 32, 86, 99, 121, 188, 192
disobedience	46, 47, 59, 186
dominion	129, 148, 150, 158
Door (the Door, or door(s)	29-33, 35, 63, 68, 161
dragon	118, 130-132, 134-135, 139
dwelling	12, 14, 26, 30-31, 38-39, 58, 74, 147, 153, 191

E

eagles (eaglets)	
bald	55,
mother	54, 79
wings like	55, 158-159,
eyes	91
Elijah	22, 93, 111
emphasis	59, 105, 163-164
enlightened (mind)	67
essence of worship	193
eternal life	21-22 58, 89, 141, 173-174
Evans (Dr. Tony)	104

F

faithful	7, 32, 37, 38, 40, 67
familiar (spirit)	161
family	
God's	21-23, 25 46, 69, 71, 108, 191
head of	99
members	95, 111, 120, 122, 192-193
Father's house	31
fear	
of enemies	97
of failure	104
of opposition	97
of death	99
of identity	106
of the Lord	165
feather(s)	55, 77, 82, 84, 98

FIFA (World Cup)	137
follow (thee)	11, 14, 34, 41, 89, 96, 178, 187
foreshadowing	55, 60
fortress	11, 15, 42, 45, 52, 189
foundation	24, 146
fowler(s)	15, 118, 119, 120,
fowler's snare	119, 125, 128
fruitfulness	58-59, 191,

G

Gate (the Gate)	23, 29, 31,
genuine salvation	16, 26, 41-42
gifts	19, 26, 189, 74
glory (God's, His)	63, 70, 49, 63-68, 70-74
God's angels	118, 122, 124-126
God's family	21, 22, 25, 65, 71, 157, 182, 191
God's household	140
God's wings	54, 56, 61, 77, 83
grow	35, 50, 87, 101, 185
growth	53, 78
grumble	12, 43, 44, 180

H

habitation(s)	18, 38-39, 41, 45,
healing	54, 71, 74, 84,
heart(s)	21, 32, 40, 95, 97, 169, 177, 192
heaven	15-16, 21, 33, 64, 68-69, 157, 189
heavenly realm(s)	16
heir(s)	157
hiding place	14, 15, 77
Holy	
Spirit	17, 21, 25, 70, 109, 143
Place	30, 33, 58, 72,
honorable	38, 146, 174-176
house	9, 26, 27, 29-35, 54, 87, 191-193
household	27, 57, 59, 140
hupernikao	135-137
Hurricanes	121
husbandry	50

I

idolatry	119, 121,
ignorance	67, 124, 135,
inhabit(s) (holy dwelling)	74
inhabitants	94, 169, 180
inheritance	70, 108, 147, 174, 175
interpret	132, 152, 166,
invitees	22
Israelites	10-12, 43, 44, 45, 54-55, 97, 159, 180

J

Jacob	58, 59, 83, 189,
Jesse	57
Jesus' brothers	157
Jesus Christ	10, 16, 23, 30, 33, 113, 138, 164, 191
joy (in the Holy Spirit)	21
judgment	45, 92, 101, 141

K

King Saul	46, 56, 106, 110, 114, 161
kingdom (of God)	20-21, 25
knowing God's name	155
knowledge	16, 20-21, 53, 69, 84, 109, 153, 186

L

largess	69
lion(s)	130, 131-134, 139
long life	13, 15, 129, 178-179, 183-184, 187, 190
love	
eternal	193
genuine	40, 152
His love	65
for God	111, 154-155
setting on God	40
upon God	151

M

mankind	11, 24, 35, 57, 93, 129, 154, 186
maturity	35, 44, 80-81, 87, 113, 173
membership	140, 182, 187
metaphors	125, 131
mind	
change of	176
confused	92
of God	12
to learn	16
renewing	167
Moses (Psalm 91)	7, 10, 12, 14-15, 26,

N

God's name	155-156
Naomi	57, 113,
new (and living way)	31-32, 147,
noisome pestilence	118, 121-122

O

obedience	22, 31, 46-47, 59, 123, 145, 186
overwhelming (victory, of victory)	136, 138

P

package	41, 44,
Panacea	103
parables	20
peace	21, 34, 37, 114, 157, 159
permanent (habitation)	45, 73,
pestilences	15
Pharisees	40
pinions	83
plagues	9-10, 15, 38, 53,
politician	152
powers	125, 133, 138, 158
Prayer(s)	
answered	46, 129
calling unto God in	111
seeking God in	111
premature (death)	154, 184

prepare (a place)	141
principalities	138, 158,
privilege(s)	147, 150, 175
promise land	12, 55-56, 82, 97, 180
prophets	13, 74, 77, 79, 80, 160, 188
Psalm 90	12, 14-15, 178-182, 184
Psalm 91	
Conditions	38
is unique	11
Moses wrote	10
secret place in	16

Q

questions	14, 43, 141, 170

R

Radiance (of God's glory)	65
realms (heavenly)	16
redemption	187
refuge	15, 31, 39,
remain (abide)	33, 52
remember (the Lord)	107-108
repentance	22, 73, 111, 140
resurrection	145-147, 156
right hand	
His right hand	140, 141, 144-145
God's right hand	139, 141-144, 149
Right hand of God	142, 143,
righteousness	
kingdom of God	21
tree of	52
sun of	84
royal (status, dominion, power)	129, 143, 150,
Ruth	57, 61, 83, 113,

S

sacred(ness)	26, 146,
Sadducees	40
saints	63-64, 82, 108, 111, 133, 142

salvation
    salvation plan of God   11, 24
    genuine salvation   16, 26
    salvation in Christ   82
    work out your salvation   23
Secret Place
    Dwelling in secret place   38
    God's secret place   9, 11,
    Of the Most High   19
    Way to the secret place   29,
seek (the Lord)   39, 112
servant   7, 22, 157, 17, 171
services (to and worship of God)   40
sether   14
shadow
    of the Almighty   14, 38, 50, 52, 73, 75, 191
    of God's wings   54, 61, 83
    of God's glory   138
shelter   14-15, 39, 46, 49, 71, 79, 80-81
snake   80, 82, 131-132, 134,
snare
    snare of the fowler   118-119, 125, 128
    devil's snare   120-121
soaring   55
Sons of Korah   25, 57
sonship (relationship)   33
sonship (right of)   133, 146
status (royal)   150
stronghold(s)   15, 47, 130
summer   53, 78, 93

T

tabernacle   19-20, 53, 64, 68
temptation   89, 120-121, 125, 186-188
terror(s)   15, 92, 98
tongues   112
tower   15, 157
translations   167
trap   119-121
treasures   34
Truth (as a shield and buckler)   86

U

under your feet	131, 133-134, 138-139

V

valleys	15
vertically	191-192
vision	80, 91, 95-97

W

Warfare	133
Way	
to the Secret Place	29
to the place	32
weapons (of fear)	47, 92-94
wedding clothes	22-23
worship	
worship experience	66
worship and glory	73
worship (of God, of Him)	40, 167
worshipping	46, 119

Y

yashab	14

Note

[1] Kathie Lee Gifford & Rabbi Jason Sobel, *The God of the Way* (Thomas Nelson, 2022), P. 45
[2] John Eldredge, *Resilient* (Thomas Nelson, 2022), xii
[3] Segun Adepoju, *Getting Unstuck*, (Cornerstone Publishing, 2021), P. 248
[4] Anthony is the first son of Dr. Tony Evans, the President of the Urban Alternative, Dallas, Texas,
[5] Jointly written by Dr. Tony Evans, Chrystal Evans Hurst, Priscilla Shirer, Anthony Evans, & Jonathan Evans, *Divine Disruption*, (W Publishing Group, ©2021 Sherman James Productions, LLC), P. 160
[6] https://hymnary.org/text/i_am_so_glad_that_our_father_in_heaven
[7] https://hymnary.org/text/begone_unbelief_my_savior_is_near
[8] https://hymnary.org/text/a_wonderful_savior_is_jesus_my_lord_a_wo
[9] More Than 4.1 Billion Watch Queen's Funeral, Surpassing Every Royal Wedding (newsweek.com)
[10] Segun Adepoju, *Getting Unstuck*, (Cornerstone Publishing, 2021) P. 222.
[11] *Supra,* @ P. 72)

Made in the USA
Columbia, SC
24 July 2023